THE ABBEY TRAIL

Clive Newsome

Published by Sigma Leisure – an imprint of
Sigma Press, 5 Alton Road, Wilmslow, Cheshire SK9 5DY, England.

British Library Cataloguing in Publication Data
A CIP record for this book is available from the British Library.

ISBN: 1-85058-803-1

Typesetting and Design by: Sigma Press, Wilmslow, Cheshire.

Printed by: Bell & Bain Ltd., Glasgow.

Cover photographs: Main – Byland Abbey; top – ford & footbridge at Ripon (day 4); middle – Kirkstall Abbey (day 1); bottom – Fountains Abbey (day 3).

Maps: the author; reproduced from Ordnance Survey mapping on behalf of The Controller of Her Majesty's Stationery Office © Crown Copyright Licence Number MC 100032058.

Disclaimer: the information in this book is given in good faith and is believed to be correct at the time of publication. No responsibility is accepted by either the author or publisher for errors or omissions, or for any loss or injury howsoever caused. Only you can judge your own fitness, competence and experience. Do not rely solely on sketch maps for navigation: we strongly recommend the use of appropriate Ordnance Survey (or equivalent) maps.

Acknowledgements

The author wishes to acknowledge the assistance of the tourist boards of Otley, Pateley Bridge, Ripon, Thirsk, Helmsley, and Whitby

Contents

Introduction   **1**
Some tips for walking the Trail   2
Places or Buildings of Historic Interest (in walking order)   5
Other Places of Interest   6

The Trail

Day 1. Kirkstall Abbey to Otley   **8**
       Distance: 11.0 miles

Day 2: Otley To Pateley Bridge   **25**
       Distance: 17.5 miles

Day 3: Pateley Bridge To Ripon   **42**
       Distance: 13.0 miles

Day 4: Ripon To Thirsk   **57**
       Distance: 15.5 miles

Day 5: Thirsk To Helmsley   **67**
       Distance: 18.5 miles

Day 6: Helmsley To Rosedale Abbey   **83**
       Distance: 16.5 miles

Day 7. Rosedale Abbey to Grosmont   **96**
       Distance: 15.0m

Day 8. Grosmont To Whitby   **107**
       Distance: 9.0 miles

Day Walks

Day Walk 1. The Washburn Valley and Dob Park   **118**
     Distance: 8 miles

Day Walk 2. Pateley Bridge, Brimham Rocks and Nidderdale   **120**
     Distance: 8 miles

Day Walk 3. Fountains Abbey and Studley Royal Deer Park   **122**
     Distance: 4 miles

Day Walk 4. Byland Abbey and Kilburn   **124**
     Distance: 6½ miles

Day Walk 5. Rosedale Abbey, Rosedale
and Old Mine Workings   **126**
     Distance: 7½ miles

Appendices

Tourist Information   **128**

Market Town Information   **128**

Map List   **129**

Bibliography   **129**

Accommodation   **130**

Car Parking   **131**

Public Transport   **132**

Introduction

A good walk can be many things to many people – it can be informative, exciting, rewarding or just plain hard work. I was persuaded to write this walk by my family and my thanks go out to Emma, James, and especially my wife Lynne for all the help during the project. I have walked many times in the Washburn Valley, North York Moors and the Nidderdale areas and I thought it would be a good idea to create a walk joining all three. These three areas each have their own character and their own natural beauty and all are good walking country.

Some long distance walks begin and end in the middle of nowhere – but a good walk should also have a positive beginning, a purpose and end. The *Offa's Dyke* long-distance path and Wainwright's *Coast to Coast* route fulfil all the criteria. They both have a coastal beginning and end, which cannot be any more definitive unless the walker wishes to swim. The purpose of the Offa's Dyke walk is to follow the defensive feature built by King Offa and the purpose of Wainwright's walk is to walk from the Irish Sea to the North Sea.

There is a lack of walks that can be completed in a week or so. Several people I have spoken to find the longer routes just too demanding on their time or fitness. My walk takes eight days – it begins at Kirkstall Abbey just outside Leeds, one of the fastest growing cities in the country, and finishes in the lovely seaside town of Whitby. The purpose of the walk is to visit seven abbeys (or priories) following ancient footpaths wherever possible. I have also tried to take in a number of old buildings on the way. Although I am an engineer by profession I have a love of ancient villages and old farmhouses and take a great delight in their architectural details.

Leaving Leeds behind gives an excellent sense of immediate achievement at the beginning of the walk and the arrival at Whitby Abbey with the splendid steep cliffs and magnificent view gives a final fantastic feeling of satisfaction.

The Abbey Trail begins at spectacular Kirkstall Abbey and proceeds via a quiet section of the Leeds Liverpool canal, out of the industrial heartland of Yorkshire to the bustling historic market town of Otley. Having travelled the Washburn Valley (Yorkshires mini Lake District) passing the reservoirs of Swinsty, Fewston and Thruscross you descend to Pateley Bridge village from remote moorland. From Pateley Bridge, the path takes us to the strange rock formations at Brimham Rocks and proceeds through the second abbey of Fountains and on to the tiny city of Ripon with its magnificent cathedral. At Fountains Abbey the grounds of Studley Royal with its famous herds of deer can be visited.

Beyond Ripon the walk proceeds to the market town of Thirsk. In doing so you will cross two rivers, the Ure and the Swale, and one major road, the A1. This is perhaps the least spectacular part of the walk but still has its own interests and excitement – crossing the East Coast main railway line without the aid of a footbridge is certain to get the adrenaline flowing!

From Thirsk you can see the Cleveland Hills and the spectacular 'white horse of Clifton' but before you gain height over the hills, visit Byland Abbey with Rievaulx a short distance away. The path beyond Rievaulx is along the Cleveland Way to Helmsley. You may pass walkers just setting off from Helmsley on the lovely trek around the Cleveland Hills. The castle and ruins are well worth a visit. From Helmsley, via rolling countryside you see historic Hutton-le-Hole and Lastingham, where St Mary's church covers the 11th-century crypt and remains of the abbey. On, then, to the small village of Rosedale Abbey (Priory). Little remains of the abbey, but a feel for the lost grandeur can be obtained from the large stone pillars left in the churchyard.

From Rosedale, by way of old mine haulage roads, we have the moorland section over the North Yorkshire Moors to the Esk Valley crossing the route of the Coast to Coast path on the way. The last section of the walk is along the Esk Valley and back up once more to the cliffs over looking Whitby and the superbly situated abbey.

Some tips for walking the Trail

Hardy walkers and those used to walking long distance footpaths can ignore this section.

◆ The walk has been broken into eight sections of various lengths averaging fourteen and a half miles per day. You choose how far to walk. Do not be set by the sections I have chosen. The very fit may walk twenty miles or more per day but those new to walking or families may choose ten miles or less.

◆ An easy way to choose how far to walk is to find a convenient point on the map at which to stop, where there is a village or small town with a telephone box. By prior arrangement, you can then telephone from this location and ask your overnight accommodation to pick you up from that place and drop you off in the morning. Most bed and breakfast establishments will do this for a nominal charge.

◆ Try to start walking with short distances and build up during the course of the walk. It is no use damaging your feet in the first few days and then walking the remainder of the path in misery. Even worse, having spent a great deal of time organising the walk only to have to pack in altogether.

◆ If you feel any irritation whatsoever on your feet stop and carry out a repair. If you can catch an area that is rubbing before it blisters, your feet will recover much quicker. I recommend a quality pair of stocks. Modern socks are purpose-made for walking and can prevent damage to feet.

◆ Try to walk in a tried and trusted pair of boots. In dry conditions, most sections of the walk could be covered in trainers – my son James still walks all his long-distance footpaths in trainers (with good grippy soles). However, they become very uncomfortable in the wet and do not give any support to your ankles.

◆ A good quality, lightweight coat is obviously essential.

◆ If you are walking with a rucksack (you can have luggage collected and passed on at some stops) try to pack the bare essentials. A few ounces can make a lot of difference over 15 miles. Remember each foot will have to be placed approximately 115,000 times during this walk i.e. 14,000 per day.

◆ The Abbey trail (at the time of publication) is a new footpath and is not waymarked as a national trail. A little experience in map reading is therefore essential. I have tried to be explicit in the text but there will always be the problem of interpretation. I would recommend a few weeks using the 1:25 000 Ordnance Survey Leisure maps before walking the trail. Do not be worried if you lose the footpath as there are generally alternatives and, as long as you proceed in the correct general direction, all will be well. It is always worthwhile carrying and knowing how to use a compass for bad weather conditions such as mist or fog.

◆ In places, the footpaths are a bit vague and a little agility may be required crossing ditches and fence lines etc. This is especially true in the area after Thirsk.

The Route

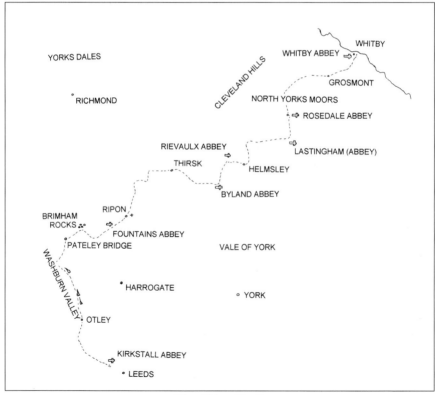

The Abbey Trail

Places or Buildings of Historic Interest (in walking order)

Kirkstall Abbey	Cistercian monastery established ca. 1250
Guiseley	Norman church of St Oswald. Rectory dated 1601
Otley	Birthplace of Thomas Chippendale. William Turner (Otley's adopted son) All Saints Parish Church and eighth-century Anglican crossed shafts described as 'the finest examples in the UK'. Many fine old buildings.
Clifton Village	Very early 17th-century farm houses
Dob Park Lodge	16th-century ruin
Swinsty Hall	Majestic manorial hall built 1627
Bewerley Grange Chapel	Built in 1494 and still in use
Pateley Bridge	Market town with fine old buildings. Nidderdale Folk museum.
Butterton Bridge	13th-century bridge
Fountains Abbey	Cistercian monastery established 1132 Fountains Hall
Ripon	Magnificent cathedral built 1220, established ca. 700. Many old buildings. 'Setting of the Watch' every evening at 9pm – a tradition continued without a break for over 1100 years. Prison and Police Museum. St Magdalene's hospital/chapel dated 1115.
Middleton Quernhow	16th-century ruined lodge
Thirsk	James Herriot's historic market town. Fine Georgian buildings.
Byland Abbey	Cistercian monastery established 1147
Rievaulx Abbey	Cistercian monastery established 1132
Helmsley	Castle built ca. 1200. Market Cross, built 1871.
Gillamoor	Magnificent historic sun dial

Hutton-le-Hole	Folk museum
Lastingham	St Mary's Abbey Church, established 654. Many fine old Yorkshire village houses. Shrines to St Cedd & St Chad
Rosedale Abbey	Ruined priory, established 1157
Rosedale Valley	19th-century mine workings
North York Moors	George Gap Causeway 19th-century stone 'trod'
Glaisdale	Water mill; Beggars Bridge – packhorse bridge built 1619
Grosmont	Main station of successful North York's Moors Railway
Newbiggin Hall	17th-century manorial hall
Whitby Abbey	Benedictine monastery established 675. Built ca. 1110.
Whitby	Old Town, Historic harbour, Captain Cook's Home, St Mary's Church built 1110.

Other Places of Interest

Otley Chevin	'Surprise View', with views as far as York on a clear day, with viewfinder.
Otley	Traditional market town
Menwith Hill	A view of the surreal 'golf balls' of the radar defence station
Washburn Valley	Yorkshire's mini Lake District
Pateley Bridge	Traditional market town
Brimham Rocks	Area of strange rock formations with tourist centre
Studley Royal	Deer park and water gardens
Ripon	Traditional market town
Norton Conyers	House and gardens
Sandhutton Aerodrome	Disused second world war aerodrome

Thirsk	Racecourse, traditional market town
Kilburn	'White Horse of Kilburn'
Wass	Tiny church with external bell
Helmsley	Traditional market town
Nawton Tower	Garden open to visitors
Gillamoor	View point
Hutton-le-Hole	Outstanding Yorkshire village, folk museum
Great Fryup Dale	Waterfalls, unspoilt valley
Grosmont	North York Moors Railway (run as a charity by volunteers)
Whitby	Marina and harbour

Mileage Chart

	Km	Miles	Leg	Total miles
Kirkstall Abbey to Otley	18	11	11	11
Otley to Blubberhouses	13	8		
Blubberhouses to Pateley Bridge	15	9.5	17.5	28.5
Pateley Bridge to Fountains Abbey	14	9	-	-
Fountains Abbey to Ripon	6.8	4	13	41.5
Ripon to Skipton on Swale	16	10	-	-
Skipton-on-Swale to Thirsk	9	5.5	15.5	57
Thirsk to Byland Abbey	17.0	10.5	-	-
Byland to Rievaulx Abbey	8.5	4.8	-	-
Rievaulx Abbey to Helmsley	5	3.2	18.5	75.5
Helmsley to Hutton-le-Hole	18	11	-	-
Hutton-le-Hole to Rosedale Abbey	9	5.5	16.5	92
Rosedale Abbey to Glaisdale	18.3	11.3	-	-
Glaisdale to Grosmont	5.5	3.7	15	107
Grosmont to Whitby	14	9	9	116

Day 1. Kirkstall Abbey to Otley

Distance: 11.0 miles

Map: Explorer 288 and 297

Refreshments: Various pubs, shops, etc

The first day is a gentle introduction to the walk, generally flat, but with much of interest along canal and river. There are many opportunities to grab a bite of late lunch at the numerous pubs or shops. An ideal place would be the Railway Inn or the Owl at Rodley. Hope for a clear day when you reach 'Surprise View' just before Otley!

Kirkstall Abbey

I spent many happy hours as a young boy exploring the ruins at Kirkstall. The extensive walls and remains of the abbey allow you to imagine what it must have been like to live in the abbey in the 12th or 13th century. With the urban sprawl of today, it is hard to imagine that the monks could catch trout by hand from the river Aire or that the abbey was sustained by agriculture. The walls of the abbey are more complete than those of any other Cistercian abbey in England. 13 monks and 10 lay brothers from Fountains Abbey established the abbey on 19 May 1152. Fountains Abbey held great sway throughout Yorkshire and its influence can be seen in many buildings in Nidderdale. The initial buildings were of wood but, after a few years, they were replaced with the start of the current structures, which were made from Bramley Fall Grit Stone. The path passes through Bramley Fall Woods after about 2 miles and the remains of quarrying can be seen by the side of the canal. Building work progressed very quickly and the cloister and its surrounding buildings were constructed before 1182. Kirkstall Abbey is probably the most impressive of the Cistercian abbeys that we see on the walk.

The monks grew rich mainly through skilful management of sheep for the quickly developing wool trade. However, by the late

Kirkstall Abbey

13th century, the monks had to seek protection from their creditors. The abbey had run up debts of five thousand pounds, a vast sum in those days. By 1301, the abbey was solvent again but the Black Death of the 14th century brought new problems and the number of brethren was reduced to seventeen monks and six lay brothers. Kirkstall was surrendered to the Crown on the 22nd November 1539.

The church at Kirkstall is unusual in that it was not rebuilt in the 13th century; it therefore retains the simplicity required by the original Cistercian order. The internal length of the church is approximately 220ft (66m), of which 200ft (60m) is unbroken, with eight immense columnar arches. The cloisters, with covered walkways where the monks and lay brothers performed their daily scriptural readings and silent contemplation, give a unique sense of tranquillity.

Old stone coffins can still be seen within the Chapter House. The main tower is not original and, in keeping with Cistercian ideals of simplicity, would only have reached as high as the church roof. The present tower was built between 1509 and 1527 but partially collapsed in 1779. Many famous artists such as Turner came to paint Kirkstall Abbey with its picturesque ruins. There is no entrance fee to the abbey although certain areas are fenced off for safety reasons.

The Walk

Set off from the abbey with the river to your right heading towards Leeds on the footpath just to the right of the main road. Pass a small building (that controlled the weir) and the miniature railway on the right, at the side of a millrace. After about 500m the path dips down to the right and crosses the millrace. Cross the bridge and follow the path round to the left on the access road to the weir building. At the end of the track at the main road, turn right. This short stretch of road is very busy but is the only link to the canal a short distance away. After the Old Bridge Inn cross the bridge (over the River Aire) and turn sharp left along the road in front of Holly Bush Farm conservation centre. You will see the Leeds University student's halls of residence, formally the Mackeson Brewery. Cross the road at the traffic lights into a wooded area and towards the canal, turn right underneath the road-bridge and follow the canal, which you now follow for several miles **(A)**.

A sign just after you start walking along the canal says Liverpool 124 miles. It must have been quite a journey for the horse drawn barges in those early days (but a better pace of life). The traffic noise is left behind as we enter the Kirkstall valley and approach the first locks. The valley is quite small and crammed into it are the canal, river and railway which at times are almost perched on top of one and other. For all late starters the canal allows you to stretch your legs and get some pace on and for the people who do not walk very often gives an ideal opportunity to wear the legs in gently. There is a good view of Kirkstall Abbey on the right. This must have been a very imposing building back in the 12th and 13th centuries. As you approach the next set of locks, the old Kirkstall Forge can be seen below. I remember being seven or eight years old and woken up on the middle of the night by the thumping of the forge (over three miles away), surely a tremendous noise at the forge itself.

The forge has been in operation for over 500 years and parts of the old forge can just be seen inside the centre of the complex. The more observant will have noticed another canal mile marker hence we have covered one and a half miles and have only another 114 to go. After 500m go under bridge 221, which carries Newlay Lane over the canal. For those thirsty walkers there is a pub just to the right called

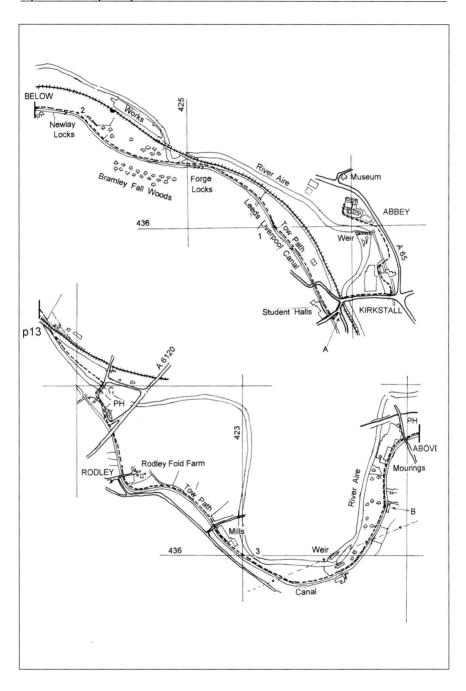

The Abbey. On the left is the mooring area for boats of all shapes and sizes and, at the end of the moorings, there is a splendid Georgian fronted building **(B)**. This section of the canal is wonderfully over-grown with a lovely sweet smell of ferns in high summer. But be-ware of cyclists!

Looking down the valley the large industrial building on the left once had the contract for the prototypes of the wind turbine towers we now see dotted around the moorlands of England, Scotland and Wales. Aeroplane modelling fans may see one or two radio con-trolled aircraft on the right at Rodley above the playing fields.

Another array of canal boats and boat yard can be seen after the Rodley Barge pub. The large concrete structure in front carries the Leeds outer ring road over the canal; here we leave the canal. Having gone underneath the bridge leave the towpath and follow the road to the Railway pub (meals can normally be obtained here).

Take the private road to the right (not the cobble track) over the lovely old Packhorse Bridge at the bottom of the slope. Grooves, worn by the continual pounding of cartwheels, can be seen on both sides of the bridge **(C)**.

At the end of the bridge turn sharp left and follow the line of the power cables. The path for the next few miles follows the line of the river, with the river on the left. At the end of the field, cross the stile and then, beneath the railway structures in front, follow the path (which can become very overgrown in summer) for about half a mile. You come out on to a track with a stone wall on the left. It is hard to believe that you are surrounded by all the major suburbs of Leeds and Bradford. Go left along the track (which can be almost im-passable in winter due to mud) and after about 300m approach a ren-dered modern brick house, take the waymarked footpath to the left. This section of the walk is part of the Leeds Country Way. Go through the gate and along the path, which again can be a quagmire even in summer (catching all the rain from the hill to the right).

Walking soon improves with the river back on the left, the occa-sional distant sound of a train disturbing the peace. Follow the river for half a mile ignoring the path going sharply to the right and even-tually just before the playing fields take the waymarked footpath across to the right.

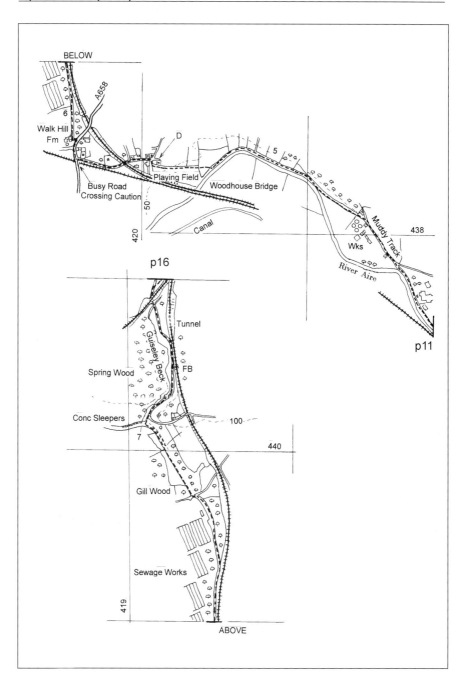

Cross the wall at the opposite side of the field into the playing fields keeping to the right-hand side with the playing fields on your left. Follow the path, eventually coming out by the side of a Victorian building **(D)**. Turn left along Woodlands Drive and follow the road for 200m until you come to the main road. At the end of Woodlands Drive, turn right up the hill and, having passed the entrance to Esholt sewage works, turn first left along a house driveway opposite the Apperley Manor Hotel. After a further 20m, turn right along the waymarked public bridleway. Esholt sewage works, to the left, is one of the biggest in Yorkshire (it is odourless however!). Follow the track through the woods for some distance with the railway line to the right. It is strange to think that if it had not been for the building of the canal and the railway (and perhaps the sewage works) the whole of the Kirkstall Valley might have been built on by now. Industrialisation has helped preserve the countryside. At the end of the track, turn left on to a tarmac road and after twenty metres turn right, heading down a track with disused sleepers and railway bed on the right.

There is a good view to the left down the Aire Valley with fields to the left and the wood to the right. After about 400m look for large pipe in front and take the track to the right heading up the hill. The little gorge to the left has an array of colour from the rhododendrons in spring and early summer. Here, you could be in deepest Derbyshire or the North York Moor valleys. Pass two large stone pillars on the left and keep on the track, going steadily uphill. Cross a bridge over a stream and underneath a railway bridge and turn right on the waymarked footpath running parallel with the railway and through a gap stile.

Follow the well-used path to the top right corner of the field, parallel with the railway into the next field. The area in front which until recently used to be open fields is now covered with a large modern housing estate. The next part of the walk is a quick dash through the centre of Guiseley.

Carry on down the ginnel, parallel with the railway; do not turn right or left on waymarked footpaths. At the end of the ginnel turn right and head down the street **(E)**. The well-manicured houses can themselves be an interesting diversion. Carry on along the footpath with the houses on the right and the railway behind the houses, looking for the footpath sign heading off to the right. Take the footpath to the right along side of No. 37 and head down the ginnel again with the railway on the right. The cars using the main Leeds-Ilkley road can now be heard in the distance.

At the main road, turn right and immediately left across the pelican crossing to head towards Aireborough Leisure Centre. Continue up the right side of the road (The Green) with the Aireborough Leisure Centre on the left and Guiseley Theatre to your right. After 200m you will come to the entrance of the Parish Church. Turn right opposite St Oswald's Terrace into St Oswald's churchyard. Built in 1150 the original church covered the area of the main chapel. It was rebuilt in the 13th century with the new St Mary's Chapel at the east-end and the tower added in the 14th century. Note the splendid late Norman doorway and excellent 13th-century transept. Inside the church there are three fragments of Anglo-Saxon crosses from the late ninth century.

Turn right around the front of the church and follow the path around to the gate at the back. Turn right down the lane and at the end of the wall left, noting The Old Rectory on the right dating from 1601. This building stands on the site of a medieval structure, the north wall of which contains Anglo-Saxon timber framework. Turn left at the end of the wall and take the ginnel up to the main road. At the end of the ginnel cross the road and take the waymarked footpath heading straight on with fields to the right and various new houses to the left. Follow the footpath, at the side of a very small stream and wall **(F)**. The direction of the path is a bit obscure at times but, as long as you follow the general direction of the small stream (or the path of it), you cannot go wrong. Through the gap stile, onto a gravel track and right back along the waymarked footpath, again following the line of the stream gradually uphill. This is good walking, soft underfoot and steady.

At the top of the field where two stones are positioned on the line of the old fence, carry straight on and across the stile following the line of the stream, between two small fences. Pass through a further gap stile heading for the top of the hill; the path follows the line of the wall and fence and zigzags left and right. Cross through the wall

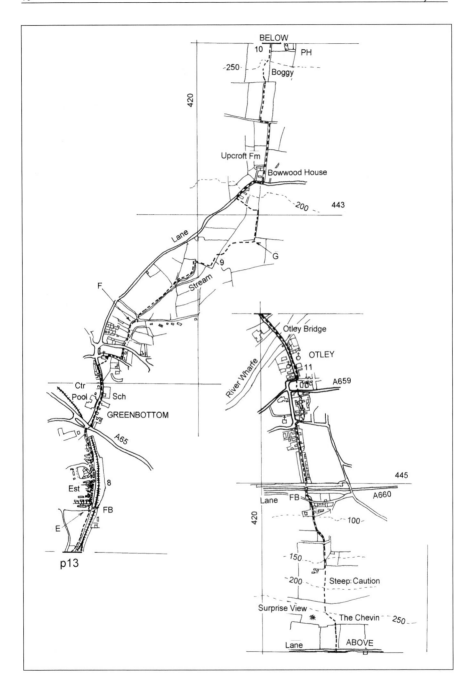

BELOW

10   PH

-250-   Boggy

420

Upcroft Fm

Bowwood House

-200-   443

Lane

9   G

F

Stream

Otley Bridge

OTLEY

11

River Wharfe

A659

Ctr

Pool   Sch

GREENBOTTOM

A65

Est   8

FB

E

p13

445

Lane   FB   A660

420   -100-

-150-

-200-   Steep: Caution

Surprise View   The Chevin   250-

Lane   ABOVE

and keep the wall and ditch to the left for approximately 100m, then follow the waymarked sign to the right, heading towards large trees. The path here is still difficult to follow. Head for a large stone in the middle of the field which used to be an old gap stile and a further stone in the distance with a hole in the middle (an old gatepost, I assume) – **(G)** . After a further 100m do not carry straight on but take the path to the left in between two rows of trees, and head for a small barn with an asbestos roof 100m in front. Cross the stile and turn left along the walled lane with a large house over to the right. After a further 150m you will enter the quiet lane heading up from Guiseley, turn right. Stay on the lane for approximately 200m until you see the waymarked bridleway to the left just after Bow Wood House. At the time of writing Bow Wood House was catering for B & B. Turn left along the track, up the gentle rise and sharp left at the top. Here, it is worth stopping to look at the wonderful views behind.

The television mast at Emley Moor (beyond Huddersfield) can be clearly seen, 25 miles away. After 70m, turn right immediately after the small barn across a stile (through a wall). Head up the field keeping the small wall on your left and through two stiles. The building just on top of the hill slightly to the right is the Royalty yet another public house which serves meals. The runway strip of Leeds and Bradford Airport is behind to the right. Carry on heading straight up the hill with the wall 30m to the right and approaching a small lane in the distance. Here, you may have to head out to the left as the ground can be very boggy .

Head for the gap stile in the top right-hand corner of the field, this leads to the car park for Chevin Forest Park. Cross the road and into the car park itself, the path at the end of the car park heads straight down to Otley. This point is called Surprise View and walkers will understand why within the next few seconds.

At Surprise View, there is a wonderful vista over Wharfedale and a plaque shows the geology of the site over the last three hundred million years. From Surprise View, you can see the market town of Otley below and, on a clear day, York in the distance. At the summit of the Chevin Steps was Jenny's Hill Cottage where in 1910, "visitors could find every accommodation to meet their bodily needs", tea was 8d or, with ham and eggs, 1/6. I can still remember the ruins, but these have been completely cleared.

Twenty metres to the right of the plaque, take the lower of two footpaths heading diagonally down to the left (beneath the rocks at the top of the hill). Halfway down the path turns sharply right and heads straight down towards Otley Town Centre. At the bottom of the grassy path cross a track going left to right, take the steep stone paved steps down the hill. This can be quite a tortuous descent for those with weaker knees, and is an ideal opportunity to test those lightweight walking sticks out. The path leads into a cobbled walled drive with the cobbles sloping slightly downhill. This can be treacherous on a wet day, although I have not slipped yet, 'touch wood'. There is a safer way, winding its way to the left, which may be better when the path is wet.

Go straight across the tarmac drive, (do not take the path to the left or right). Pass a stone walled Victorian house to the left and a modern bungalow to the right. Carry on down the path, eventually coming out to a road. Cross the road and take the path heading diagonally to the left, at the side is a small holding with a menagerie of animals. Cross the footbridge (the road was originally the route of the railway line down the Wharfe Valley and is now the Otley bypass) and carry straight on down the cobbled road. At the bottom of the modern steps was the old Otley Station, now demolished. The road is, of course, named Station Road. Otley is blessed with many wonderful cafés and pubs, and the hungry traveller will not have any problem in finding something to eat.

At the bottom of Station Road turn slightly right and cross the road, heading down the ginnel at the side of the Woolpack. Over to the left is All Saints Parish church with its eighth-century crossed shafts. The building behind you was the home of Chippendale. Turn right behind the Woolpack and immediately left, heading into the centre of Otley, with lots of small interesting shops on both sides. The famous Black Bull Pub is at the end of the street on the left. Turn left after the Black Bull and then immediately right through the market place and through the ginnel called Bay Horse Court, at the side of the Bay Horse Public House. The ginnel comes out on to Clapgate. In front is the site of the old Royal Oak Pub (now a solicitor's office) built in 1651 with the old Prince Henry's grammar school building over to the left. Head down Bridge Street.

Just before the river is the Wharfe View Café – a favourite eating place of mine – frequented by cyclists, walkers and bikers. A friendlier café would be hard to find, serving good grub and a lovely pint pot of tea to a wonderfully eclectic group of customers.

Otley

Otley is a busy market town and is still influenced by the farming community. The town still has its cattle market and auction house, which appears to be flourishing. On the way into Otley, you pass All Saints Church, which has a striking collection of Anglican crossed shafts. This testifies to the Christian community in Otley from the 8th century. Later history is evident by the fascinating effigies, tombs, brasses and tablets dedicated to the Fairfax family of Denton. One of the crosses is known in the academic world as probably the finest carving in the whole of the Anglo-Saxon period. North of the churchyard, another unique monument records that 23 workmen were killed while constructing the Bramhope Tunnel in 1845.

The Market Square of Otley retains its old cross and many old buildings, which have not been spoilt by the sixties rebuilding madness. There are lots of ginnels, interesting small shops and an enormous number of pubs, too many to count. Otley has its market day on Friday and Saturday. On the north side of Otley, the old bridge crosses the wharfe. This area is a hive of activity in the summer with boats on the river and children playing in the park just beyond. Otley is well worth a longer visit if you have the time. Why not visit the museum at Otley? It has such artefacts as tools that date back 12,000 years. In addition to its natural attractions, Otley has become a magnet for those interested in the arts or history. Turner, Chippendale and Wesley are three of its better known patrons and attract tourists from all parts of the world. Otley's contribution to the growth of the printing industry, its historic carnival and Victorian Fayre and the annual Arts Festival are additional reasons to visit Otley. There are facilities in plenty for the walker. Cafés, inns of historic interest, restaurants (some mentioned in international Food Guides) and fast food shops all cater for the palate.

Mankind has occupied the valley of the River Wharfe and its surrounding hills for centuries. The Iron Age culture awaited the

Romans, when they marched north to create York in AD71. The name of the river is probably Celtic in origin and there are other place names that attest to long residence of the Celts around here. A number of coins discovered in the locality attest to at least a limited Roman occupation of the site after the third century AD but Otley as we know it today did not appear until the Anglo-Saxon period.

When King Edwin of Northumbria annexed the tiny Celtic kingdom of Elmet around AD616, it is probable that Otley was part of a larger settlement. Local legends speak of Otley church being founded by Edwin's Bishop Paulinus. There are some impressive Anglo-Saxon stone cross fragments attesting to the importance of the parish in Anglican times. By the time of the Norman Conquest, the little township had gained the name of *Othelai* – though the origins of the name are not at all certain. A century or so earlier, the Manor of Otley had passed, together with the Manors of Cawood and Wistow, into the ownership of the Archbishop of York. The three areas were part of a gift granted to the church by King Athelstan in 937 as thanks for his victory in the battle of Brunanburgh. The remains of a house and chapel built by later archbishops can be seen behind the present Manor House in Manor Garth Park, overlooking the river. After the Norman Conquest, the 'borough' of Otley seems to have grown rapidly, being significantly larger than nearby Bradford by the reign of Richard II. We also know that by 1265 the area was sending two members to Parliament.

The Fairfax connection may well have been the reason for Otley's parliamentary leanings during the English Civil War. Denton Hall close to Otley, was the home of the Fairfax family and the birthplace of Thomas Lord Fairfax the Parliamentary General. Allegiances may have been split for, while Roundheads were drinking the town dry in the night proceeding the Battle of Marston Moor, legend has it that Prince Rupert's cavalry horses were out to grass on the lower slopes of the Chevin.

Progress went on unhindered in Otley. A new bridge was built to replace one almost destroyed by a flood around 1672 and Prince Henry's grammar School was founded in 1607. The leading light of Methodism, Charles Wesley, had a long connection with the district. In 1718, Thomas Chippendale, Otley's most famous son, was born. Towards the end of the century, J.M.W. Turner, the renowned landscape artist, began his long association with the district.

At the start of the 19th century, Otley had a population of just over 2,000. This had risen to 9,000 by the end of the century, with sixty-one different public houses to cater for increased demand. Connection with leather, paper, and the printing machine industry flourished during the Industrial Revolution. Otley's Railway Station disappeared in 1967 and a contraction of its industrial base gradually followed over the next two decades. It is interesting to note that plans have been put forward to restore the railway through to Otley within the next few years. Otley now prospers as a tourist location (now with twenty-seven pubs). This has been partly assisted by Yorkshire Television's 'Emmerdale Farm', sequences of which are filmed in Otley. More recently many episodes of 'Heartbeat' have been filmed here.

Thomas Chippendale

This celebrated cabinet-maker, is probably Otley's best-known son. He was born in Otley in 1918 and baptised in Otley Parish Church on 5th June of the same year. He was the son of John and Mary (nee Drake) Chippendale, the family being joiners by trade who lived in a small house in Boroughgate. Long since vanished, the site of the house is commemorated by a plaque and an inscription in stone on the walls of Building Society Chambers, Boroughgate. Thomas's mother fell ill when he as ten years old and he was sent to live with his uncle Joseph, a school teacher and his father's youngest brother. The house was of white-washed sandstone with a thatched roof. Now faced and roofed in stone, the cottage still stands and is at present the Cobblestones Tea Rooms (at the bottom of Station road) and is also marked by a commemorative plaque. Mary Chippendale died in the February of 1729. Although he did not live at home, Thomas worked alongside his father and served his apprenticeship in Otley. It is known that they worked together at nearby Farnley Hall and, during the early stage of his career, he made the famous Doll's House at Nostell Priory.

In 1793, Mr Henry Lascelles purchased the Harewood Estate, six miles east of Otley, out on the Arthington Road. The Chippendales made furniture for the owner, from oak grown on the estate and it was in this way that Thomas's genius became recognised by the Lascelles family. They encouraged him to consider working in London where his craftsmanship might well appeal to the nobility. That it did is now part of history.

Sad to say no example of Chippendale's art exists in Otley. Perhaps the finest authentic examples of his furniture in the area are to be seen at Harewood House just six miles east of Otley and at Temple Newsam House in Leeds where the collection of the Otley-based Chippendale Society is housed. The Chippendale Society was founded in 1963 with the aim of promoting interest in the life and work of Thomas Chippendale. In 1968 to mark the 250th anniversary of his birth, an avenue of 170 trees were planted on Otley Chevin and in 1987 a bronze statue, was erected to his memory in Manor Square. The famous son of Otley has returned to the streets than he knew so well as a child.

William Turner

Joseph Mallord William Turner, although born in London can be regarded as an adopted son of Otley. Turner made his first visit to Yorkshire in 1797, when he was 22; he had been commissioned by the Lascelles of Harewood to paint watercolours of the area. So attracted was he by Otley and its surroundings that he returned time and time again and, on striking up a friendship with Walter Ramsden Fawkes, became a very regular visitor to Farnley Hall, two miles from Otley. Fawkes was to be Turner's greatest admirer, patron and friend and continued to buy his paintings, especially watercolours done in the vicinity. The two men became very close, spending their leisure time riding, shooting and fishing together on the extensive Fawkes estate, which took in a large section of Otley Chevin and stretched as far as Menston. At that time, the Chevin boasted deer, goats and wild boar, while the Wharfe and the Washburn were brimful of trout and grayling.

Turner left behind a complete pictorial record of life at Farnley Hall and the surrounding Otley area. He sketched the Washburn, Bolton Abbey, The Strid, Barden Tower and deer being hauled down in triumph to Caley Hall. It is said that his magnificent portrayal of

Hannibal crossing the Alps is based on his sketches of a storm across the Chevin.

Turner continued to visit Farnley Hall each year and Fawkes continued to be a generous patron. However, when Walter Fawkes died, these visits ended. Nevertheless, as Ruskin, the art critic, said "Of all his drawings, these of Yorkshire have the most heart in them, the most unwearied, serious, finishing truth". Turner is as indebted to Otley as Yorkshire is to him.

Places of Historic Interest

Otley retains many of its older and more interesting buildings, chief amongst them being All Saints Parish Church in the town centre. Standing on a site that has been used for worship since Saxon times, this church has a nave, aisles, transepts, chancel and West tower. It dates from the 11th to 15th centuries although it was twice restored in the 19th century when the present font, screens and choir stalls were added. The pulpit and altar rails are of the Georgian period. Of great interest in the churchyard is a memorial to 23 men who died building the nearby Bramhope Tunnel on the Leeds to Harrogate and Thirsk railway line. Recently refurbished it is an exact replica of the north portal of the tunnel. Also of note are a gravestone of an ancestor of the poet Longfellow and a monument to an 18th-century member of the Fawkes family from Farnley Hall.

The market place is, in spite of the distractions of modern day bustle, a place for quiet reflection on how things used to be. Alongside the Market Place is the Buttercross, which was built to replace an ancient cross. The Buttercross is not a cross at all but a Dutch barn with wooden seats. Until 1939 it was used by local farms to sell their produce, the right to do so going back to mediaeval times. The tradition is kept alive by local charities that hold small fund-raising events there on a weekly rota. Otherwise, it is just a pleasant idiosyncratic public shelter. Part of the original Buttercross can be seen outside the north door of the Parish Church.

Adjacent to the Buttercross is the Jubilee Clock. Completed in 1888 by public subscription at a cost of £175, it celebrates Queen Victoria's Golden Jubilee. Its fussiness is typical of Victorian design and, in true Victorian tradition, it has four faces and no chimes so that it can be 'seen and not heard'. The clock bears tablets that recall two Otley men killed in the Boer War; it also commemorates the hospitality received by Belgian refugees during the First World War.

A few metres from the clock you can see one of Otley's oldest inns, the Black Bull dating from the 16th century. It still supplies refreshment and succour to thirsty travellers just as it did during the Civil War when a party of Cromwell's Ironsides arrived and, legend has it, drank the place dry the night before the Battle of Marston Moor.

Otley Methodist's church has examples of carved mice in the woodwork by the world famous 'Mousey Thompson' of Kilburn (see day 5).

Day 2: Otley To Pateley Bridge

Distance: 17.5 miles

Map: Explorer 297 Explorer 298

Refreshments: a pub on the A59, half a mile off the path

This section is a long day's walk up the Washburn Valley past three major reservoirs and over the moors to Pateley Bridge.. There is a pub at Hopper Lane (half a mile off the path) which sells food at most times, but that's it, so a packed lunch is almost essential.

Cross the river and head uphill out of Otley towards Blubberhouses. The Victorian houses on the left must have been positively palatial back in the late eighteen hundreds when they were built.

Keep heading up the hill past the Yew Tree Pub on the left and past the Wharfedale General Hospital with its restored but austere Victorian frontage (my wife thinks it's pretty).

Just after Carr Bank Bottom and opposite The Gills turn left off the road towards a garage **(A)**. Just past the gable end of the garage is a footpath beneath large sycamore and oak trees with a ditch and small brook to the left. Cross the stile and follow the footpath heading up the left-hand side of the field, now leaving Otley well behind. Keep following the path near the left-hand side of the field. A lovely view of Wharfedale can be seen to the left with a glimpse of the Cow and Calf rocks above Ilkley in the far distance.

At the very top left-hand corner of the field, cross the stile and head at 90 degrees to the wall up a slightly raised path across the middle of the field. (Head slightly to the left of the communications tower on the top of the hill.) At the top of the field, enter a gravel track through a metal gate, with a stile to the right and then through another stile and gate leading diagonally up the hill on the track to Clifton.

Pass through two gates into a tarmac lane, perhaps taking a last look at Otley before heading over to the Washburn Valley. Enter Clifton Village, another one of my favourite little hamlets, and take a few moments to look at some of the wonderful old buildings. The mullioned windows of the first farm are almost completely covered by ivy. The next two farms date from the mid-1600s, the date stone being difficult to decipher. The upper windows of Old Hall Farm are also covered in ivy. Both this building and the next have lovely details over the windows and one of the buildings dates from 1604, very early indeed. The row of cottages at the top of the hill dates from 1744. Keep following the tarmac lane past the old church, successfully converted into a house, now approaching virtually the top of the hill with the communications tower in front. At the end of the lane turn left back onto the Blubberhouses road, cross the road and immediately after the entrance to Maverick Farm take the waymarked footpath into the field to the right **(B)**. Cross the wall and keep to the left hedge-line along the field. Cross the next stile and head diagonally to the top corner of the field past the barns on the right. Cross the stile and head along the farm track on the right-hand side of the next field. After crossing the next stile, keep heading in the same direction with the fence immediately on your right.

Almscliff Crag can be seen over to the right and the Wharfe Valley in the distance. Cross the stile, and keep heading in the same direction with the first close up views of the Washburn valley. A waymarked post can just be seen to the left in the far corner of the field where the fence joins the stone wall. The large communications mast to the right can be seen from most points over the next two days. Cross the stile and onto the tarmac lane and head right along the lane going slightly downhill past two houses on the right, the first of which would appear to have unusually low pitched stone roofs. Turn left along the track towards Dob Park House. The next section of the walk crosses some of worst stiles I have ever come across – I hope these will be improved in the near future.

Look for a stile on the left, and after 50m climb the next stile to take the detour round Dob Park House. Round the corner you will see the first glimpse of Menwith Hill with the surreal "golf balls" of the RAF communication centre seen on top of the hill. Through the next stile and gate and on to a lovely grassy drove road **(C)**.

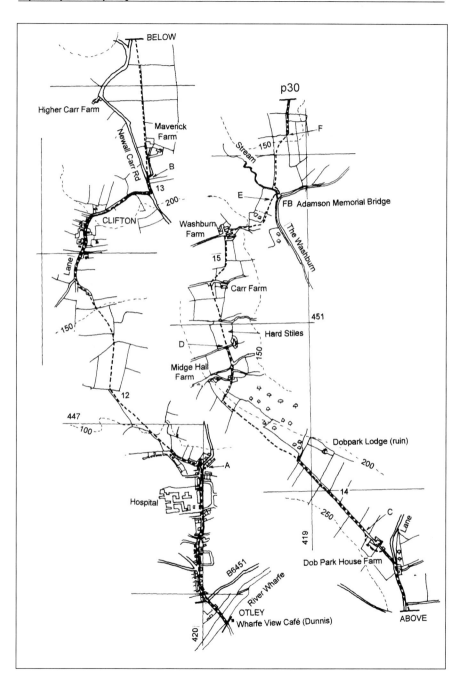

From this point, there are wonderful views of the Dales and the hills above West End with Nidderdale over to the right. Towards the end of the drove road are the romantic remains of Dob Park Lodge. The first view of Swinsty Reservoir can also be seen over to the right.

At the end of the drove road cross the stile and keep heading in the same direction parallel with the wall to your right. The wall eventually dips away but head in the same direction across the full length of the field, aiming for the point where the wall ahead meets the tree lined hedge. This is lovely soft walking: ideal for those who are breaking in tender feet.

Carry on over an old wooden ladder stile into the next field keeping to the left-hand hedge/fence. Cross the next stile and turn sharp right down the field heading towards a small farmhouse in the bottom, look for a stile and a gate with a waymark sign. Through the stile and gate then take the path to the right of the farmhouse following the waymark sign. After a few metres turn slightly left and over an old clapper bridge across the stream and a stile into a walled drove road (do not go through the gate). Go over another stile and cross a track (leading down to an old ruined farm complex) through a gate and into the next field, following the line of telegraph posts **(D)**.

Follow the waymarked stile over the stream and head away from the right-hand wall towards a ladder stile and a barn to the left. Go over the next three stiles and on to the farm track. Take the ladder stile into the field opposite and follow the path down towards the next farm, heading for the corner of the field (directly in line with the reservoir beyond). Cross the next ladder stile and head down towards the farm complex, keeping the wall immediately to your left. The complex is comprised of two farms and, as the farm tracks converge, turn sharp right and down the adjacent drive, with a stone barn to your left. Look for a waymark sign on the very end of the barn.

Go over a stile in the wall and head down the field to the left of a green painted wooden barn, looking for a waymark sign in the wall to your left. Keep heading down the field but slightly to the left, going round a copse of trees surrounded by a broken-down stone wall. At the bottom of the copse turn left and up the valley looking for a waymark sign on a small oak tree to your left. Go through a broken-down wall and head slightly to your right. Look for a waymark sign on one of the trees on the embankment to your right **(E)**.

Take the path downhill to the stream and cross the Arthur Adamson Memorial Bridge. A very unusual and tiny imitation packhorse bridge built by the Ramblers Association. Having crossed the bridge turn *sharp left* and follow the stream for about 100m, then right heading uphill following the wall to your left, do not carry on along the path at the side of the steam. The path goes sharply uphill heading for the gap at the top right-hand corner of the field.

At the top corner of the field go through the gap in the wall (to the right) and follow the left-hand wall **(F)**. Eventually go through a gate into a walled farm track and on to a farmhouse on the left. Head straight through the farmyard and proceed in the same direction along the walled lane and through various gates/stiles. This next section of path can be boggy at the best of times – so beware.

After 500m, the path comes to the side of a wood just above Swinsty Reservoir. Pass through yet another gate and look for the Yorkshire Water Authority sign indicating the entrance to Swinsty reservoir. Turn right and head down into the woods. After about 100m take the path going diagonally down to the left, signposted 'permissive footpath' and then turn sharp right in front of Swinsty Hall. Swinsty Hall is a beautiful building dating from 1576, with lovely feature windows, doors and chimneys etc. note the finials to the tops of the gable ends.

Having passed Swinsty Hall, turn left at the bottom of the track on to the access road. Follow the track up to the car park at the head of Swinsty reservoir embankment.**(G)**. From the Swinsty Moor Plantation car park take the road signposted to Otley and Timble; do not take the small lane up to Timble itself.

At this point if time is pressing or you prefer a simple walk through to the A59 at Blubberhouses, there is a permissive path at the side of Fewston reservoir. This starts opposite Swinsty car park with a single path that comes out in the car park at Blubberhouses so you cannot go wrong.

Follow the road for about 200m to the first house on the right and take the waymarked footpath signposted Blubberhouses Road, after

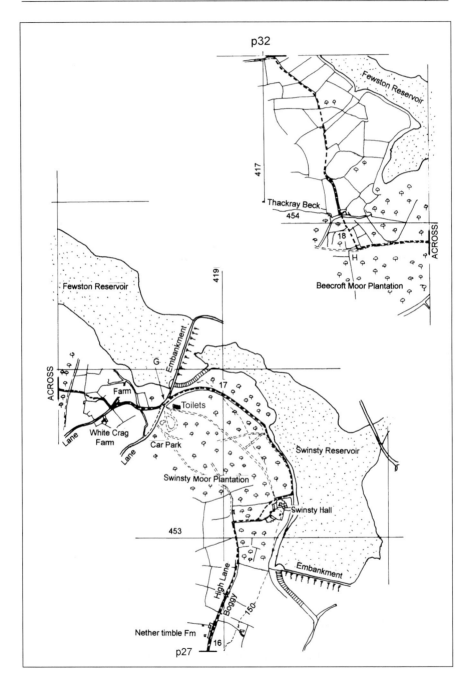

p32

Fewston Reservoir

417

Thackray Beck

454

18

H

ACROSS

Beecroft Moor Plantation

419

Fewston Reservoir

Embankment

G

ACROSS

Farm

17

Toilets

Lane

White Crag
Farm

Lane

Car Park

Swinsty Reservoir

Swinsty Moor Plantation

Swinsty Hall

453

Embankment

High Lane

Boggy

150

Nether timble Fm

16

p27

the house. Follow the path, or the line of the wall to the right, to the top corner of the small field or enclosure. Go through the gate and head along the footpath with the wall to the left, through a gap stile and along a track into the woods straight ahead. Follow the track for about 500m (ignoring a track to the right) then look for a broken-down wall on the right. About 25m after this wall turn right into the woods, this path is difficult to find so keep checking your map **(H)**.

Head down through the woods coming out by a stream, a nice place for a picnic on a summer day. Cross the bridge and the stile and head up the small lane in front. At the top of the walled lane, head slightly left and through the gate with the yellow waymarked sign. Follow the wall around to the right and then the line of the fence for about 150m. Here, head left across the field to a gate where a long wall meets a tumble down wall. Cross the stile and carry on in the same direction to the right of the small section of wall in front. Cross another stile then follow the line of the wall on the left, going through the left of the two gates in front. Follow the path with the wall to the right, into the next field. Just before the corner of the field, take the ladder stile to the right and follow the line of the wall on the left, with Fewston reservoir to the right. At the next corner, cross through the broken-down wall and head for the ladder stile with Blubberhouses church in front **(I)**.

Head down the hill towards the busy Skipton/Harrogate road (A59) and over the stile into the car park.

Turn left into the car park and right just at the end of the bridge, through a small gap stile on to the road. Taking extreme caution, cross the road and at the far end of the bridge go down the bank onto the permissive footpath. The footpath follows the line of the stream up to Thruscross reservoir (completed 1966) and West End.

After 400m, Blubberhouses cricket ground is passed to the right, which was the site of a large mill; the mill leat and impounding dam can be seen to the right as you walk up the valley. Follow the line of the stream for approximately one mile. Cross a footbridge on to the left bank of the stream. Take the track up to the left towards the trees and away from the stream. After a few metres the path joins a track (coming down from the left). Turn sharp left then immediately sharp

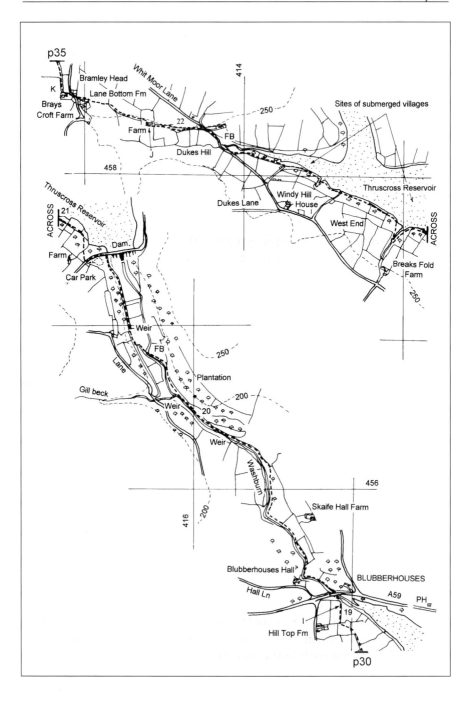

p35

Bramley Head

Whit Moor Lane

414

K

Lane Bottom Fm

Brays
Croft Farm

Farm

22

250

Sites of submerged villages

FB

J

Dukes Hill

458

Thruscross Reservoir

ACROSS

21

Thruscross Reservoir

Dukes Lane

Windy Hill
House

West End

ACROSS

Farm

Dam.

Breaks Fold
Farm

Car Park

250

Weir

FB

Lane

250

Plantation

Gill beck

200

Weir

20

Weir

Washburn

456

Skaife Hall Farm

416

200

Blubberhouses Hall

BLUBBERHOUSES

Hall Ln

A59

PH

I

19

Hill Top Fm

p30

right over a stile, then right along the tarmac track towards the dam. After 300m, just before gates, take the footpath sharply left up the hill heading for the left-hand end of the dam.

Turn left on the road and up the hill for approximately 150m. Opposite the entrance to the car park, turn right on to the permissive footpath along side Thruscross Reservoir. Simply follow the waymarked path along the side of the reservoir for the next mile. This is easy walking with no stiles or gates and only the occasional jumping of fish to disturb the peace.

To the right, the old village of Thruscross is submerged in over 30m of water. At the first little inlet, the old tarmac road used to go down to Thruscross village and can be seen coming out on the far side. There are some lovely pictures of old Thruscross in the book by 'Alred'. As the reservoir narrows, the old village of West End lays submerged also. When the reservoir is very low which happens quite often, it is possible to walk along the bottom, over the old packhorse bridge and past the ruins of the old houses and church, a very strange and sad experience. The church was left standing when the reservoir was first impounded but was later demolished. Yorkshire water authority said this was due to safety reasons, but the locals say that it was due to the sound of ghostly bells heard coming from the sad empty church.

Continue along the path until the very end of the reservoir. Here, the path circles round an embankment, all that remains of the old reservoir that served West End village. Leave the water board land via a gap stile and turn sharp right (not on to the road). Take the path down the side of the fence and across the footbridge in the bottom at the side of a small waterfall. Enter the road and turn right up the hill and as it bends round to the right head left through a gate and along a track with a small wall to the left leading slowly downhill. Follow the path with the bottom of a bank just to your right (having passed three stone troughs) and approach a unusual farmhouse with a mixture of period architectural styles (J).

At this point, there is a slight diversion from the O.S. map. Cross the small ladder stile in front of the house, turn right through a gate, passing the gable of the house and turn left. Look for a stile in the wall (the line of the path in the next field can be seen in the contours of the land). Go straight ahead and through a small gap in a partially dismantled wall, towards the farm in the distance. The path continues to the right-hand side of a line of trees, crossing a farm track and over a stile. Head towards the right corner of the barn, the path skirts round the barn with the barn on your left.. Head along the side of the farm buildings (but not on the farm track) and then via a step stile onto the lane at the end. Turn right along the lane and then left into the next farm.

As soon as you enter Brays Cross-farm itself, turn sharp right and with a further barn on your left follow the track behind the farm buildings. After about 60m, take the waymarked track up to the right **(K)**. Follow the track to the top of the hill where fantastic views can be seen in all directions. On the horizon to the left is Rocking Hall on the 'Dalesway' link from Harrogate.

The next section of the walk can be rather tricky to follow with the added difficulty of a stream to cross in the bottom of the valley. As you walk along the walled track at the top of the hill, look across the valley to the right and there is Humberstone Farm in the woods, with a white-topped barn just to the left. This is the general direction to follow over the next mile or so.

At the end of the track enter the next field and keep in the same direction with the wall to your right. Cross the stile in the end wall and the farm track and go through the gate in front (just to the right of three stone pillars). In fog or mist I would suggest that you follow the lane to the right and then left on to the main Blubberhouses to Greenhow road – soon turning right into High House Farm and back onto the path. Head down the middle of the field towards a gap in the wall. Go through the gap and look very carefully in the left wall for a step-stile between two posts **(L)**.

This is not the easiest of stiles to cross but, having successfully negotiated it, turn right and follow the line of the wall on your right for 100m. There is no clearly defined path and it is simply a case of heading in the general direction of the farm (you can still see the top of the roof over to the left). If you look carefully, you should see a depression in the ground indicating the track. Never mind about the direction too much as long as you are heading for the stream in the bottom. At a point 50m down stream of where two streams join, you

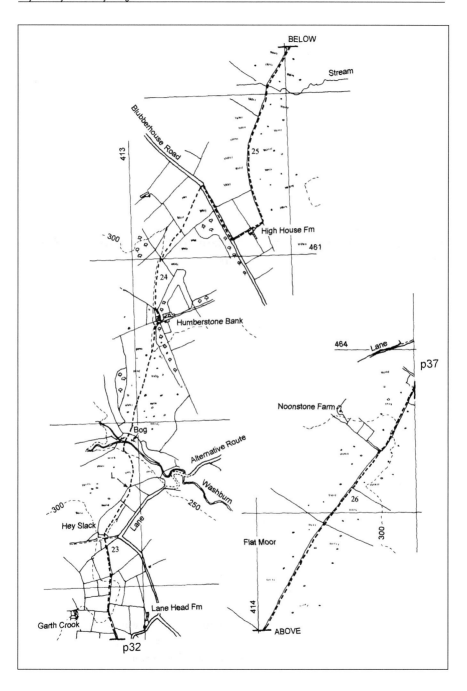

will see a small gate in the stone wall on the opposite bank, this is the direction to head for. The stream can be crossed here although it can be quite difficult. The area between the stream and the gate in winter is a bog and has to be skirted round, but in summer you can walk straight across.

Go through the wall and head perpendicular to it and up the hill. Again there is no well-defined footpath, especially in summer when the bracken is at full height. As the gradient flattens out, head for the left end of the line of trees on the horizon. Take the gate through the fence (just before the wall) and head towards the barn, keep the wall to the right and then turn right towards the house through two gates. Turn immediately sharp left down the side of the barn through two further gates and into the field at the far end of the paddock and head for the left of two gates.

Head parallel to the right-hand wall to a further gate in the distance. Through the gate, head up to another gate slightly to the left and just to the right of a small ditch. Turn right through the gate on to the Greenhow/Blubberhouses road. Walk down the main road for about 300m to the entrance to High House Farm, left up the farm drive along the waymarked path. Carry straight on up the farm drive to the left of the farm. Go through the two gates and out onto the moor, keeping straight ahead until the end of the next small field. Turn left and generally follow the wall for the next few miles over the moors towards Pateley Bridge.

For the first 400m the route is not very clear and the simplest way is to follow the line of the wall to the left.

After a short while the well-worn track can be seen in the distance following the wall line. There is a series of grouse butts at the side of the path. The side of the Nidderdale Valley can be seen at last and the small copse of trees on the horizon waymark the Cleveland Hills. At the top of the hill over to the right Yorke's Folly (a Victorian imitation ruined castle) can just be seen overlooking Pateley Bridge. Brimham rocks are across the valley.

After almost a mile go through a gate and down the track. Shortly after the gate, the welcoming sight of Pateley Bridge can be seen. Where the track starts to bear left at Ravens Nest carry straight on down the green footpath and pass through the narrow gap stile at the

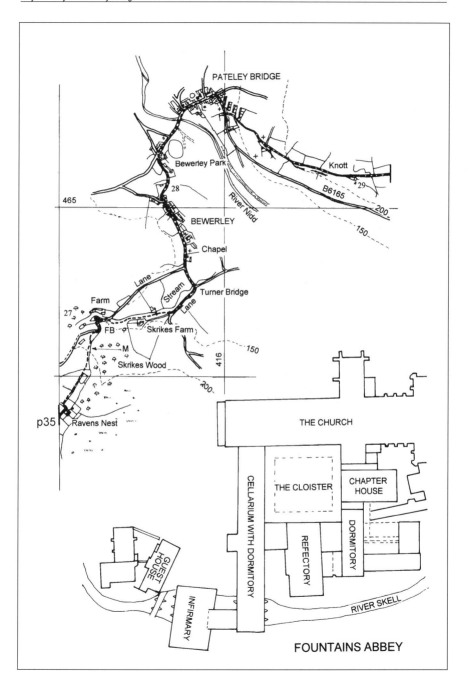

PATELEY BRIDGE

Bewerley Park

Knott

B6165

29

465

28

River Nidd

200

BEWERLEY

150

Chapel

Lane

Stream

Turner Bridge

Farm

Lane

27

FB

Skrikes Farm

150

M

416

Skrikes Wood

200

p35

Ravens Nest

THE CHURCH

THE CLOISTER

CHAPTER HOUSE

CELLARIUM WITH DORMITORY

REFECTORY

DORMITORY

GUEST HOUSE

INFIRMARY

RIVER SKELL

FOUNTAINS ABBEY

side of the gate. Head down a grassy walled lane to the track at the bottom, turn left along the track for about 30m and take the stile through the wall to the right. Walk down the field, keeping the wall to your right and heading for a stile in the wall at the bottom of the field.

Be prepared, this next section is a very short but very steep descent **(M)**.

The footpath descends parallel with the right-hand wall and as the wall curves away to the right go straight on to the lane via a gate. Take the lane down to the right past the farm on the left and turn right immediately before the little bridge at the bottom. Enter Skrike's Wood, cross a small footbridge and follow the path to the left. Keep following this footpath along the stream, coming out onto a lane after 400m. Turn left and head down the hill. At the road bridge and junction of the lanes take the left-hand fork signposted 'Pateley Bridge (¾)'. Carry straight on, past Peat Lane and into Bewerley. Bewerley Grange Chapel on the right must be visited (see text). Follow the road through Bewerley to the main road, turn right down the hill into Pateley Bridge. Pateley Bridge is blessed with many tearooms and pubs, most of which serve meals.

The Washburn Valley

Lindley Wood Reservoir

Lindley Wood was the first of the Leeds Corporation reservoirs in the Washburn Valley it was built between 1869 and 1875 to meet the growing population of Leeds. The navies who constructed the dam had their village below Greystone Beck. Some 35 buildings were constructed including brick huts, a wooden church, a beer house and store and a school, which eventually became a smallpox hospital. On the 6 October 1871 30 cases of Typhoid were reported.

The dams of Swinsty and Fewston soon followed the construction of Lindley Wood. Fewston was built between 1874 and 1879 and has a capacity of 4,350 million litres. Swinsty has a capacity of 4,800 million litres. Fewston village was a thriving community until the construction of the reservoir. The construction of the dam changed the water pressure in the subsoil and resulted in massive structural failure of a substantial number of buildings in the village, most of which had to be demolished.

Dobpark Lodge

The Vavasours of Weston Hall built this around 1600. The castle was probably the centre of a deer-park but by the late 18th century the lodge was already a romantic ruin sketched by Turner in 1816.

Swinsty Hall of Little Timble

Little Timble is a small-detached township of the York Archbishops estate and dates from pre-Conquest times. The two farms of Nether Timble and Swinsty Hall are the only remaining houses on the ancient manorial holding. To the north of Swinsty Hall, and alongside the Washburn, was New Hall – the home of Edward Fairfax, author of *A Disclosure of Witchcraft* (1621). Fairfax claimed that his daughters, were bewitched by local women but his claim was rejected on two occasions in 1622.

Swinsty Hall has been described as the best, most substantial, most majestic of all the old halls in the Washburn valley. Among its many features the hall has rooms and windows some bearing the initials and the date HRG1627 as you would imagine there is much oak panelling and great open fireplaces with a carved oak gallery. One interesting feature of the construction is the stone benches in the main entrance. These were hollowed-out stoops and held ale in which coins were placed to disinfect them during the great plague.

Fewston

In the 1800s Fewston was well-populated with a saddler, a baker, blacksmith, butchers, grocers, cobblers plus the Smiths Arms Inn. During the construction of the reservoir the population was swelled by the navies and the village was said to be alive as never before or since.

The church at West End existed from the 1500s and in 1873 the existing building was renovated and became the Parish Church. By 1880 there were only eight families left in the ruined village of Fewston. The demise of the buildings had become a sad public spec-

tacle. It was said that the builders of the village had an eye more for
the picturesque than for the solid as they had built the houses on a
continuously active landslip. However, construction of the reservoir greatly increased the damage to the buildings. The decaying
buildings were transported for construction work elsewhere; the
crumbling Cragg Hall at the end of Busky Dyke Lane was removed
and re-erected stone by stone at Hollyhill Huby in 1957.

Bewerley Grange Chapel

The chapel was built around 1494 as part of Bewerley Grange be-
longing to Fountains Abbey. The granges were occupied by lay
brothers and served as centres for wool collection and other local
produce. A Cistercian statute of 1152 insisted that the granges be no
more than a days travel from the monastery. The granges prospered
and acquired more land and labour until the Scottish Raids of 1318
when Fountains became the Scots base for a few days. A document
dated 27th July of that year referred to the granges and outside places
as destroyed.

It is likely that King Edward II spent the night at the adjacent ab-
bots lodgings here on 23rd September 1323 so there must have been
considerable rebuilding in that period. By the mid-14th century, the
granges were tenanted. When the Chapel was built (under the super-
vision of Marmaduke Huby, the 31st Abbot of Fountains) the
Darnbrook family held half of the lodge of Bewerley at an annual
rent of £8

Huby a great builder had a favourite motto "SOLI DEO HONOR
ET GLORIA" (Glory and honour be to God alone), used on Fountains
Abbey and on the east wall of the chapel with the initials M H below.
At the Dissolution, there were five tenants. Bewerley was sold in
1522 to Sir Arthur Darcy and 20 years later Bewerley manor was sold
by Darcy to Thomas Benson. The lease included the monastic chapel (now used as a house)

As a point of interest the coat of arms of the Norton's of Norton
Conyers can be seen in the chapel (they were great benefactors of
Huby and the abbey) and the Abbey Trail passes their family home
after Ripon

Pateley Bridge

Pateley Bridge is a quite little village/town nestling between the steep hills of the Nidderdale Valley. Old mine shafts and ruins of smelt mills are dotted around the surrounding hills towards Greenhow and further up the Dale. Lead has been mined in this area since Roman times. The railway once reached Pateley Bridge and was opened in 1862 to serve the lead mines and flax mills and with hopes of encouraging tourism. It finally closed in 1964 and its route can be traced with a footpath following a good section of the track up and down stream of Pateley Bridge. Pateley Bridge has a steeply sloping main street with old buildings on both sides and some interesting antique and craft shops. There is plenty of accommodation and B & B's abound. Not far from the main street is the Nidderdale museum, which has a large collection, illustrating all aspects of Dales life.

Day 3: Pateley Bridge To Ripon

Distance: 13.0 miles

Map: Explorer 298

Refreshments: Pub at Sawley. Café at Fountains Abbey Visitor Centre

A shorter day's walk than yesterday, passing through rolling farm-land and leaving time for a visit to Fountains Abbey or a walk around the deer park at Studley Royal. Again, there is little opportunity to purchase food although there is a café at Brimham Rocks (check opening times). There is a pub at Sawley but (as I point out later) it is not really geared up for walkers, so the safest bet is a packed lunch.

From Pateley Bridge head up the main street and round the cor-ner on to Ripon Road, walk along the left-hand pavement to just be-yond the church and turn left up steps signposted 'Panorama Walk'. The next section of the walk, until just before Brimham Rocks, fol-lows a section of the Nidderdale Way.

At the cemetery carry on walking steeply uphill. This lovely sec-tion of the walk has views over the lower Nidderdale Valley. As the path flattens out between the modern house on the right and the farmhouse on the left, carry on in the same direction along the tar-mac road, then bear left on to the track waymarked Nidderdale Way. The track shortly turns into a grand walled, path (again with pan-oramic views down the Nidderdale Valley).

As you approach a track coming from the left, bear right heading slightly downhill eventually leading out on to the Ripon road. Turn left and walk uphill **(A)**.

After about 200m turn right in front of a row of terraced houses again signposted Nidderdale Way and after 400m (bearing right at rock house) onto a small lane. Turn left up the lane and as the lane bears sharply left carry straight on down a walled path, which after 100m comes out (crossing a small stream) onto another lane. Turn

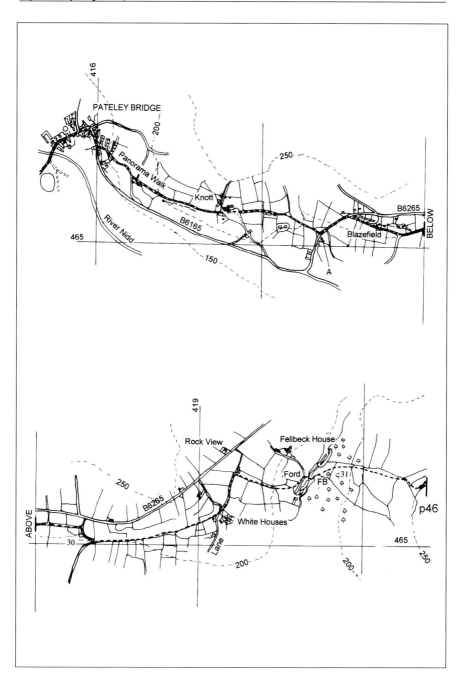

right down the lane and after about 150m, as it hairpins to the right, turn left through a stile.

Looking up the steep embankment to the left you can see millstone grit rock, which forms the wonderful sculptures of Brimham Rocks a short distance away. Through another stile just above a bungalow and take the path leading slightly up to the left. Come out, after half a mile, above a collection of farms and houses known as Whitehouses. Carry straight on (ignoring the paths to the left and right) down a walled lane with a small house on the left (parts of Brimham Rocks can be seen to the right). After about 200m as you approach the first house, take the waymarked footpath to the side of the house and over a stile heading downhill. The unmistakable noise of peacocks can be heard from a very long way away off and anyone wishing to see them can take a short detour through the stile to the left and down to Felbeck House. Numerous peacocks give wonderful displays most of the year.

Go through the stile and follow the left-hand wall down the next field, taking the first gap through the wall to the left and heading onto a farm track. At the end of the track, turn right down the hill and across a footbridge over the river by a ford. Here we leave the Nidderdale Way and take the small ladder stile to the left. Follow the track uphill on the left side of the field, noting that one of the fence lines has been removed and is not as indicated on the map. Do not take the waymarked path through the wall to the left, (neither of the paths to the left) but carry on heading uphill through two gates. Keeping the fence to your left, carry on heading uphill until, at the top left-hand corner of the next field, cross a stile into a walled 'sheep crush'. As the walls open out turn sharply right. Carry on steeply uphill and cross a ladder stile. Head diagonally up to the left onto the farm track and exit North Pasture Farm complex by the track.

At the top of the track, take the stile heading uphill towards the rocks. Having crossed the stile the official route of the path goes diagonally to the right up through the woods, (note the view behind). It is very difficult to follow and perhaps the best route would be to carry straight on with the wall on the left, a path following this same general direction can be picked out working its way steadily uphill.

As the path splits, generally take the right-hand fork to the bottom of some quite impressive boulder rocks. Follow the path beneath the rocks and then head up when possible to a large path at the top of the hill. Turn right along this wide path, which eventually leads to the visitor centre and café.

As mentioned previously, paths in this area are very difficult to follow but as long as you head steadily uphill, you will come to the main path. Brimham Rocks are a popular place for amateur climbers and families enjoying the pleasant surroundings and wonderful natural rock formations. This is also a favourite spot for bilberry picking

Leave on the main track with the café to your left. As the track bends to the right go straight along a path down the shallow valley in front. There are so many footpaths in this locality that it can be difficult to find the intended route. For those not so hot at map reading, it may be better to follow the main track down to the road and then turn left **(B)**. Having followed the path to the best of your ability, come out onto the road and turn left. Fantastic views can be seen of the Vale of York and the Cleveland Hills. Where the road dips down slightly a sign indicates 'National Trust No Parking farm access only' take the concrete paved track down to the right across the cattle grid and into the next field. Cross a further cattle grid to the complex of houses. Follow the road through and, before a modern house, turn left through the gate. Follow the line of trees down the field and through a gate **(C)**. Although the waymarked sign indicates straight on, there is a rarely used footpath heading ninety degrees to the left. Less intrepid walkers may prefer to walk on the waymarked footpath down to the road and back up towards Middle South Farm. Having passed through the gate follow the wall / fence line to the left for about 70 metres and then head diagonally to the right, the path can just be seen heading down to the stream in the bottom. Head up the hill through the woods. After 50m, pass through a small gap in the wall on the right into a field. Follow the wall on the left up the field with South Farm 100m to the right. Cross the remains of a stile into the next field with the hedge now on your right. A stile can be seen in the top right corner of the field.

Turn left into the lane and at the 'T' junction after Middle South Farm, turn right. As the lane bends round to the left notice the

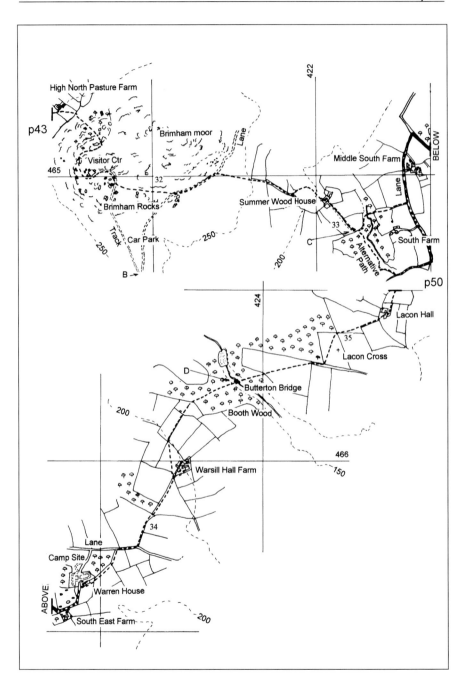

Christmas tree growing out of the top of the stone pillar! As you approach a camp site, and before the first caravan on the left, turn right into the paddock. Follow the path around the back of the complex of houses and then behind the caravan park itself, coming back on to the road. Turn right onto the road and after about 150m, turn left along the waymarked footpath heading to Warsill Hall Farm. Follow the fence line down the field heading for a green gate in the wall. Through the gate follow the wall line and down to the farm track. Before the farm, just by the top barn turn left through the gate, and after about 30m turn right through the gap stile. Head diagonally across the field to the gate in the far corner with a white house beyond.

Go through the gate and head down the field with the wall to your right. Pass through the next gate and then, through a small gate in the wall and right down into the woods, eventually crossing the 13th century Butterton Bridge in the bottom of the valley **(D)**. The bridge was built on the route between Fountains Abbey and the outlying Granges of Pateley Bridge. Butterton is derived from 'Butterdene' (ca1216) meaning 'Valley with rich butter-producing pasture'. Hav-

Butterton Bridge

ing crossed the bridge and a track, head straight up the hill into the woods. Alternatively walk about 50m to the left and then up the forestry track. Having crossed through the gate at the top of the hill head diagonally to the right, there is no proper footpath but you should be heading for the end of the row of trees on the horizon. Cross the stile and, at the end of the wood, turn left over another stile into the field. Head diagonally to the far right-hand corner passing the remains of Lacon Cross, a 12th-century signpost. A view of Harrogate can be seen to the right and Ripon in the far distance.

Cross the stile and head downhill to a further stile into the gardens of Lacon Hall noting the huge chimney-breast for such a small house. Follow the track past the houses and, 100m after a cattle grid, having crossed a small bridge over a ditch, bear left to a stile in the top corner of the field. Go over a stile and head for the far right corner, past an electricity post. Cross the next stile and carry on heading in the same direction over a further stile into Sawley Moor Lane, then turn left on the main road into the centre of Sawley.

After the church, turn right down Low Gate Lane. Refreshments may be had at the Sawley Arms but the menu is not really for the average walker. More Egon Ronay than eggs and chips!

Walk down the quiet lane for approximately half a mile and, after a short distance, you will pass the old farm at Hog Hall. As the lane bends round to the right, and by a sign for Low Gate Lane, take the waymarked footpath into the woods. This section of path has now been adopted by the City of Ripon as the Ripon Rowel Walk. Cross the river by means of a little packhorse bridge and then turn right onto the forestry track, now making a beeline for Fountains Abbey. The track comes out via a stile to the lane just up from Fountains Abbey. Here, there are three options: those with time on their hands can carry on down the road to the right and pay the fee into Fountains Abbey and water gardens; those wishing to see the deer of Studley Royal can walk up the road to the left and bear right up to the Fountains Abbey Visitors Centre – carry on up the path to the church and turn right following the Ripon Rowel through Studley Royal and back to the path (dotted on map). The route that I have chosen, however, is quiet throughout the year and gives a good panoramic view of Fountains Abbey. It is probably best for those with limited time on their hands. Therefore walk down the road to the right bearing right past the entrance to the abbey and Fountains Hall, following the road going slightly up the hill signposted 'Harrogate 12' with a car park on the right.

Having walked 100 metres it is interesting to note that the sign now says 'Harrogate 9' you never knew you could walk so fast did you. Follow the road up the hill with the abbey wall on your left, some of which is in an excellent state of repair after nearly 800 years, a tribute to the craftsmanship of the masons of those days. About three-quarters of the way up the hill there is a good view of Fountains Abbey. Take the first stile on the left hand side and follow the line of the abbey wall into the fields for about 400m.

The abbey must have been very wealthy to be able to build such extensive perimeter walls. The wall of course built for privacy and not for defence. Go through the gate in the perimeter wall and down the fenced footpath towards Hill House Farm. Turn right at the bottom of the field and through a gate following the waymark signs and farm track to the entrance to the farm. Through the farm gate and turn right on to the paved area in front of the barns and then left around the end of the barns following the waymarked signs into the field and following the hedge line.

Head downhill towards a wall and the gate in the bottom corner of the field. The path follows the line of the wall to Studley Royal, passing an imposing gatehouse in a poor state of repair. Please note the section of wood you are now walking through is called Robin Hood's Wood. He seems to get everywhere! **(E)**

After about half a mile, the path heads left and downhill. Go

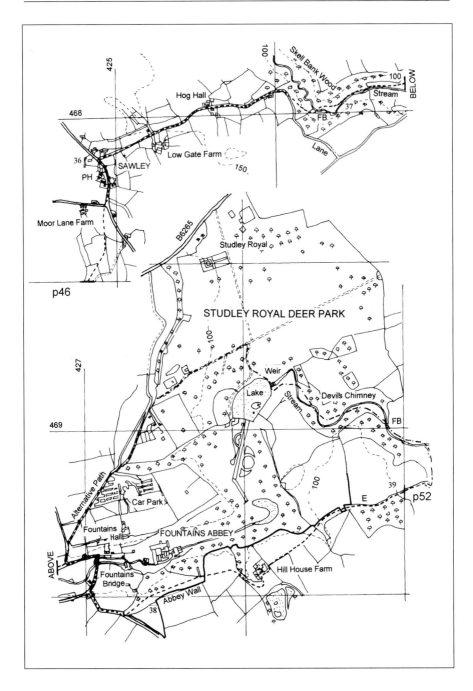

straight on and take the signposted path to Ripon. Those people having walked through Studley Royal would rejoin the path here **(F)**. You are again on the route of the Ripon Rowel. Exit the wood via the small gate and join the well-used footpath across the field. The outskirts of Ripon can be seen in the distance.

Follow the path down past hawthorn trees and a fence line to a gate and then left into a small lane. Ripon Cathedral can be seen in the distance standing out quite splendidly among the trees. Follow the lane for just about half a mile towards a new estate – Ripon, like all towns in the country, is spreading. You now have a far better view of the Cleveland Hills in the distance and the plain that we have to cross tomorrow before reaching them. Just after the end of the wood on the left (with the houses about 400m in front), take the footpath to the left – keeping tight to the left boundary of the field. Follow the hedge line round to the side of Hellwath Cottage. Turn left and then turn immediately right into the footpath beneath a hawthorn hedge (a tunnel formed in Hawthorn). Where the path splits, keep to the left heading down towards the River Skell. Follow the Skell for the last mile into Ripon. After about half a mile go down a flight of steps at the side of the river and pass a footbridge on the left. Carry on the right hand bank of the Skell leading on to a tarmac lane between Georgian houses before the main road. Turn left and pass through the play area, having perhaps sneaked a quick dip in the paddling pool. Leave by the gate on the far side again with the river on your left, under the road bridge on a gravel path coming out on to the road.

Turn left into the road with the new flats on the left and cross the road bridge 'built in 1993', into Williamson Drive and follow the waymarked sign through the new housing complex to the city centre. Turn right at the top of the lane into Water Skellgate and immediately left up Duck Hill. After 100m, you are in the busy centre of Ripon and the market square.

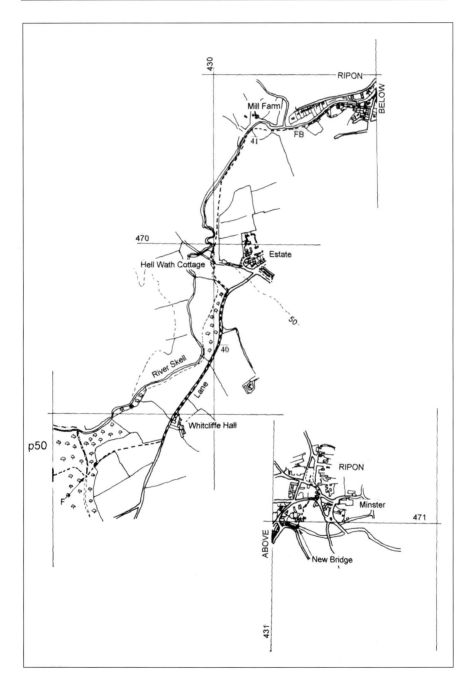

430

RIPON

Mill Farm

BELOW

FB

41

470

Estate

Hell Wath Cottage

50

40

River Skell

Lane

p50

Whitcliffe Hall

RIPON

Minster

471

F

ABOVE

New Bridge

431

Fountains Abbey

The Cistercian abbey of St Mary's is one of the most beautiful of all monastic ruins. It was one of the earliest, largest most celebrated of communities in Britain. Its early history was developed through 13 monks of the Benedictine abbey of St Mary's York who in 1132 objected to the lack of discipline. After a violent struggle the thirteen monks, along with Archbishop Thurstan, moved to the Archbishop's estate at Ripon where land was granted to build a new abbey. Wooden huts would have been used initially and fresh water would be obtained from the many springs (fonts) from which the abbey eventually took its name. The initial years spent in establishing the abbey on uncultivated land must have been very hard. By 1135, the monks were on the point of despair, when they were joined by the wealthy Dean of York. The Dean brought money and lands to the new community and further benefactors came forward, which helped the abbey prosper.

In 1135, work began on more permanent stone buildings. By 1150, Fountains had sent out 91 monks to begin six new abbeys in England and Norway. During the rule of the third Abbott, Henry Murdac, severe problems were encountered due to in-fighting among the local Archbishops and the Papacy. The result was that the King's son, Fitzherbert, raided Fountains and burned parts of the structure, thereby inflicting great damage. Surprisingly the Abbott Murdac was missed in the raid – 'protected by the hand of the Lord'. Rebuilding began at once and the abbey soon grew in fame. By the end of the 12th century, there were more than 200 lay-brothers and in excess of 50 monks. Much rebuilding was carried out under three Abbotts in the early part of the 13th century and, by 1291, the abbey's annual revenue was more than £356. Raiding parties caused considerable problems in the 14th century and the Black Death of 1348 saw a sharp drop in the number of lay-brothers.

By 1380, 34 monks remained and a few as 10 lay brothers. Fountains became a 'mitred' abbey (one given special status by the papacy) and there was a further period of building in the quarter century before and after 1500. After the Dissolution, which began in 1538, the abbey was surrendered on the 26th November 1539. The King's Commissioners seized ornaments and vestments to the sum

Fountains Abbey

of seven hundred pounds as well as almost 2,000 cattle, over 1,000 sheep, 86 horses, 79 swine and 221 quarters of various grains.

At the Dissolution, the abbey and much of the property was sold to Sir Richard Gresham and later sold to Steven Proctor. Fountains hall was built by Proctor out of the remains of the abbey. The church at Fountains was very long and narrow extending to over 350ft (106m) with a nave of 11 bays and north and south transepts. The *cellarium* (a larder for the storage of food and wine) is still extremely impressive even today with our ability to use modern materials. It was built in the late 12th century and is over 300ft (90m) long with twin aisles of 22 bays and 19 internal columns all with ribbed vaulting an absolute masterpiece and still in wonderful condition.

Ripon

Ripon is one of the smallest cities in England. Many ancient customs are still proudly preserved through this great city and one such is that of the Ripon Hornblower. The Hornblower appears each night at 9.00 p.m. to sound his horn at the four corners of the Obelisk, at the centre of the market place.

The long-standing ritual is known as 'Setting the Watch' and originally assured the citizens of Ripon that they were safe in their houses for the night. It has continued without any break whatsoever for over 1,100 years. Day to day activities in Ripon are centred on the large marketplace, surrounded by an outstanding selection of Georgian and medieval buildings. Other sites of particular interest include the half-timbered Wakeman's House and the Town Hall. The obelisk that was first erected in 1781 took the role of a market cross, and stands in the centres of a busy market, which takes place every Thursday.

Ripon's greatest glory – indeed, the jewel in its crown, is undoubtedly the Cathedral. This is one of Yorkshire's finest treasures and stand, in all its splendour, at the end of Kirkgate.

Particular point of interest include the fascinating St Wilfred's Saxon Crypt, the spectacular West Front and, in the Cathedral Treasury itself, an exhibition of ecclesiastical silverware. Other special features are the Tudor library, art nouveau pulpit, medieval screen and 15th-century choir stalls.

Ripon Cathedrals west front, built in 1220 by Walter de Grey Archbishop of York is one of the finest examples of the early English style of architecture. The cathedral was built on the site of St Wilfred's early Saxon church of ca AD700.

The pews at Ripon Cathedral have more examples of Robert 'Mousey' Thompson's work. The world-famous wood craftsman from Kilburn made pews with his mouse trademark.

The church of St Mary Magdalene was built in 1115. It was founded by Archbishop Thurstan of York to care for lepers and blind priests. The church is normally locked but the huge key can be obtained from an adjacent house.

Ripon Races are a fine day out with 14 racing days every year. The Policy and Prison Museum in St Mary's Gate houses a fascinating collection of exhibits illustrating the history of law and order in the city. This marvellous building dates from the year 1686, when a House of Correction was first established. The city's newest museum dedicated to the Yorkshire Poor Law is housed in the 1877 Ripon Workhouse in Allhallowgate.

Annual events include the two-week Charter Festival in late

May/early June and St Wilfred's Procession in August. The latter
fills the streets with a cavalcade of floats to celebrate the safe home-
coming of said saint from his exile in AD 686. The procession culmi-
nates in a rather special service at the mighty Cathedral.

The recent restoration and re-opening of the Ripon Canal and Ba-
sin now makes this the most northern point in the connected water-
way system of England and Wales.

Day 4: Ripon To Thirsk

Distance: 15.5 miles

Map: Explorer 299and 302

Refreshments: Pub at Melmerby

This is the flattest part of the walk, from the Eastern Yorkshire Dales, to the borders of the North York's Moors. Walking between 30m and 40m above ordnance datum (the average sea level at Newlyn in Cornwall – AOD for short), the scenery is perhaps the least dramatic of the whole walk, but excitement is achieved in the crossing of both the A1 and the East Coast main railway line – gulp! Again, there is little to be had by the way of food. The pub at Melmerby at the time of writing only sold crisps and the small post office at Sandhutton has recently closed, although there is a pub. So it's a packed lunch – cheese again!

Today we have to cross the Ure, the A1 and the Swale. Because of the flat open nature of the land there are very few intact paths most of which have either been taken up by country lanes or have been swept aside by the numerous aerodromes and farms etc. This gives a very limited choice of route in this area.

At the bottom corner of Ripon market place take the road down Duck Hill and after about 70m bear left down Kirkgate towards Tourist Information and the Cathedral, with a splendid view of the west front. Take the path to the right of the Cathedral, passing through the old graveyard. Follow it through the grounds to High Saint Agnesgate, turning left and then right into Low Saint Agnesgate. Carry straight on down towards the river. Do not cross the river, but turn left on to the gravel path and follow this for about 200m, turning left by the ford onto the road and then right into Granger Row. At the end of Granger Row carry straight on beneath the railway arch, now the Ripon bypass, onto a track. Follow the waymarked footpath signs by the side of the river, leading into fields

Ford and footbridge across the River Skell

beyond. For the next mile, the path follows the side of the Ure back to the busy road junction where the A61 meets the Ripon Bypass.

As you pass under the new bypass keep towards the left-hand abutment and follow the path onto Albion Terrace/Magdalene's Road. I recommend a visit to the hospital-church of St Mary Magdalene (built in 1115 to tend lepers). It is 200m along Magdalene's Road to the left. The key can be obtained at the house adjacent to the church. Turn right again onto the A61 road-bridge and cross to the left where possible. At the end of the bridge by the roundabout turn left again along the road towards the camping and caravan site. After about 150m, the road branches. Take the left-hand branch along Urebank Terrace for 400m where the road has been partially closed by a ground collapse.

The ground in this area is subject to catastrophic failure due to undermining by water erosion, holes open up without warning. At no 24, the whole garden has disappeared and the house has been abandoned. Carry straight on down the track, with the river to the left, and follow the riverbank and a line of stakes for half a mile until the river bends to the right. Go over a stile by the side of a gate and keep to the left with the football pitches to your right. Head for the corner of the field, at the side of the embankment; take the path up the embankment, following the fence line **(A)**.

Go through the kissing gate at the corner of the caravan site and walk along the field with the trees to your left, through another kissing gate on the right and up onto the old railway embankment. At the top of the embankment, turn left. Head back in the original direction and, after a few metres, descend onto the road and turn left. The next mile and a half are a bit of a road slog, through Nunswick towards Norton Conyers, although the road is very quiet. Before Nunswick cross the tiny but grandly named Kings Bridge. Nicely mown grass verges on this section can give some relief from the hard surface. You can see the house at Norton Conyers (of Bewerley Grange connection) in the distance through the wood. The historic house and gardens of Norton Conyers can be visited throughout the year, entrance times should be checked with Tourist Information. The original Norton family, including the sons, were executed for rebellion against Elizabeth I. A later owner, Sir Richard Graham, was a supporter of Charles I and died from wounds sustained at the battle of Marston moor. Cromwell followed the dying Graham back to Norton Conyers and took vengeance by destroying the interior of the building.

A sign giving details is passed at the southern-most entrance. Two hundred metres after this, where the house wall bends left, take the waymarked footpath across the field to the right, signposted to Melmerby. To the right the land is called Whinny Hills – a strange description for the land at this point that is only 35 metres AOD and some five metres *lower* than Melmerby in front.

Follow the line of the hedge to the bottom corner of the field, through the hedge and over the footbridge into the next field. Pass a brick farmhouse on the left, which looks as though it has been extended in recent years. The extension has been built to absolute perfection to match the original building. At the top left-hand corner of the field, follow the waymarked stile across the next field looking for a stile through the hawthorn hedge. Follow the left-hand hedge line of the next field through to the track at the end and then between the

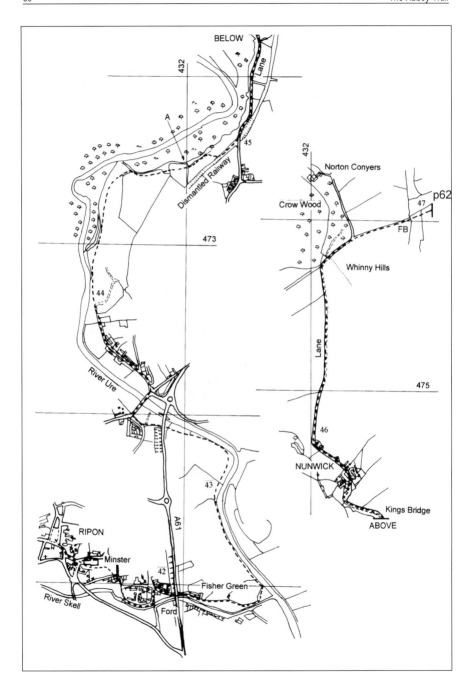

bungalow and the mock Georgian house and into the tarmac lane towards Melmerby. Turn right at the end of the lane onto the main road into the centre of Melmerby passing the George and Dragon public house. Although the sign says 'bar meals', meals are not served at lunchtimes.

As the main road turns to the right take the small lane to the left signposted 'Middleton Quernhow' (meaning 'mill hill') for approximately a mile. Ignore the turnings for the A1 and Wath and take the left turn (after Old House) to Middleton Quernhow itself. Middleton Quernhow is a sleepy little village with the romantic ruins of a once extensive manorial hall. The owner of the hall Sir Thomas Herbert had royal favour of Charles 1. The hall has been abandoned for a long time and, according to an old directory, its remains were occupied by a humble cottager in 1840. Follow the road round to the right and back out of the village. Cross the lane and take the narrow tarmac lane directly for the A1, this tarmac lane turns quickly into a track. At the end of the track is the very busy A1. *Please* take extreme care crossing this road – take your time, gaps *will* appear **(B)**. The only quiet time on the A1 is at about 3 o'clock in the morning, which is not a good hour to be walking!

Cross the road and take the path slightly to the left, via a farm gate. The waymarked sign can just be seen in the hedge on the corner of the field. The plot of land to the left was the site of a recently demolished public house,. Leave the A1 behind and walk down the field keeping the hedgerow to your left. At the bottom of the field, follow the waymarked sign onto the right side of the next field (in the same direction). Keep following this general direction with the hedgerow to your right for the next four fields (ignoring the path to the left after the third field) with Skipton on Swale over to the right. Go over the stile and right at the waymarked sign, following the quite busy road for 400m down to the bridge at Skipton on Swale. At the end of the bridge, take the ladder stile to the left – heading slightly back on yourself – and over two further stiles. Turn sharp right, again following the hedge to your right do not follow the flood defences parallel with the river. The nicest route here would be to follow the levy at the side of the Swale but there is no public right of way.

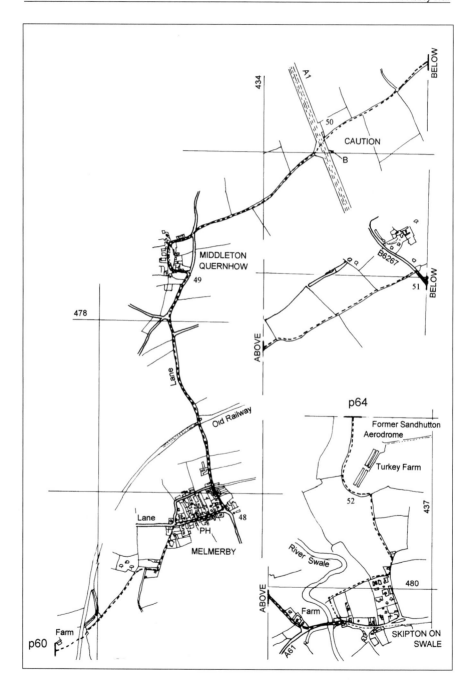

Pass through two fields and then three gates with a large barn and old airforce buildings on your right. Turn left down the access track after the small brick house to the old aerodrome. The aerodrome is primarily used for arable farming and turkey farming. The turkey farms are built on the remains of the old runways. Turn left onto the perimeter road. After about 300m, it was my original intention to follow a footpath by the side of the Swale and then right onto Foss Sike Lane. However, the footpath has completely disappeared over the years and the barbed wire fences makes this option impossible. The alternative is therefore to keep following the aerodrome access road round to North Turkey Farm, turning off along Foss Sike Lane, perhaps at some point the County Council will open the blocked footpath. The perimeter road however does allow good uninterrupted views of the Cleveland Hills.

Just after North Turkey Farm, there is a large green storage tank on the right. About 100m after this turn left down a track, then immediately right onto Foss Sike Lane Track (path) towards Sandhutton (a welcome relief from the tarmac of the aerodrome). At the end of the track turn right and then left at the Kings Arms into the centre of Sandhutton, a pleasant village with some lovely Georgian brick houses.

Follow Sandhutton Lane past the church on your right for about one mile, passing Mowbray Farm on the left (yet another turkey farm). As the road turns ninety degrees to the right, you can see a waymarked footpath sign to the left, just after a new house called Stone Cross **(C)**. Turn left down the access road and after about 100m, follow the waymarked footpath through the hedge into the field and round the left-hand corner of the field to the caravan site, crossing the footbridge. Follow the path around the caravan park, through the woods and then back away from the caravan site, across the middle of the field with houses to your right.

The path crosses the main north/south London to Edinburgh railway line, which is to say the least a bit intimidating. As with the A1 just take your time, look carefully and remember the trains are travelling at over 120 miles per hour. At the end of the field turn right onto a track and then after 50m left across to the gap in the hedge. At the railway line turn right for 50m and take the ladder stile onto the

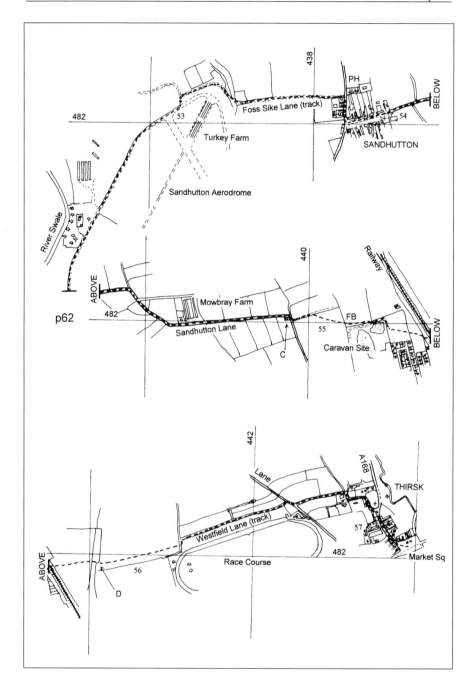

railway property itself. Head straight across the tracks to the stile directly in front of you on the far side, (sometimes overgrown – trust me, it is there). The next footpath is not particularly well used but you should be generally heading for the wood slightly to the right in the distance, to a gap in the hedge. Go through the gap and follow the footpath 50m to the left of the right-hand hedgerow, heading towards the church tower in the distance **(D)**.

We are now heading for Westfield Lane about 100m from the top right-hand corner of the field. Leave the field and carry on down Westfield Lane with the tower of Thirsk Parish Church of St Mary in the distance. At the end of the track turn right and then after 50m turn left down Cemetery Road towards the church. Follow the lane past the cemetery and church, down into the town centre, turning right at the main road. Thirsk has many nice little cafés and pubs in its small market square.

Thirsk

Thirsk has a long and varied history with Romans, Saxons, Vikings and Normans all occupying the site. Situated in the Vale of Mowbray under the Hambleton Hills, Thirsk is conveniently located for visits to the Yorkshire Dales.

The *Domesday Book* of 1086 records that Thirsk had two Manors with several plough teams in each, also ten villeins (freemen with shared fields). About this time, the Manor of Thirsk was given by William the Conqueror to one of his Barons – Robert de Mowbray. This family dominated the region for approximately 400 years and the name of 'Vale of Mowbray' is still in common use. Robert built a castle to the west of the present Market Place which was entirely of wood as no evidence has been found to suggest a stone building. A number of the de Mowbrays took part in conspiracies against Henry II but, on each occasion of their defeat, they were pardoned. The King needed strong Barons in the north to resist the invading Scots. However, in 1184 Henry II ordered the destruction of northern castles, including that of Thirsk.

Thirsk church took 70 years to build, being started in 1430 and is described as the most spectacular perpendicular church in North

Market Square, Thirsk

Yorkshire, often been called the Cathedral of the North. Near to the church is Thirsk Hall – a fine Georgian Mansion. Originally built in 1720/1723, it was later enlarged in 1771 to the design of John Carr of York, who added a third storey to the centre block plus two wings, each of two storeys. The Hall is occupied by the Bell family, the first Lord of the Manor being Ralph Bell, appointed in 1772. Up to 1772 the Bell family had occupied 'The Old House', which can still be seen on Front Street, Sowerby.

Thirsk was also the home of James Herriot, the famous vet and author of many wonderful books such as *All Creatures Great and Small.*

"Thirsk I would say is a happy town. It has a cheerful aspect with its cobbled square and its fretted line of roofs set off by the long ridge of the Hambleton Hills. It has an abundance of good shops with smiling people behind the counters and some splendid inns with welcoming landlords." James Herriot

Day 5: Thirsk To Helmsley

Distance: 18.5 miles

Map: Explorer 302 Outdoor Leisure 26

Refreshments: Café at Kilburn. Pubs at Byland, Wass, Kilburn and Bagby.

This is the longest day of the whole walk and there may be little time to visit Byland and Rievaulx abbeys. It may be worth considering splitting this section of the walk into two if you wish to visit both abbeys properly. With the exception of the climb out of Byland, the walk is fairly flat. Good progress can be made on the latter stages of this section over well-waymarked footpaths, although the first mile after the A19 is hard going – I suggest allowing an extra half hour for map reading and hedges! Just before Kilburn there is a good view of the 'White Horse'. There is a pub and café at Kilburn, both of which are most welcoming, there are also pubs at Byland and Wass but it is a good idea to check opening times.

Leave Thirsk on Finkle Street, past the library and the bridge over Cod Beck. Turn right along the waymarked footpath through a garage forecourt. Through a kissing gate, take the smaller footpath immediately to the left following the line of the hedgerow, do not go diagonally across the field.

Proceed through various kissing gates heading in the same general direction for 300m coming out to the corner of the field onto the main road by a large factory. Once you see the factory head towards a bungalow and the corner of the field towards a waymark post by the road. Cross the road and follow the waymarked sign in front of the blue building and across the cricket pitch to a position roughly to the back of the side screen. The path is unclear here but you must cross the ditch and onto the bottom of the A19 road embankment heading north along a very infrequently used footpath at the gable end of the factory.

The next mile can be very frustrating due to the poor waymarking – so please take your time and study the map.

Go through a gate and turn right to an underpass beneath the A19. Turn right through the gate at the end of the underpass and again fight your way through the undergrowth, to head south. After 150m a stile can been seen in the fence with a track opposite; at the time of walking there was no footbridge across the ditch and there has to be a scramble up the far bank to cross the stile. Take the track towards the middle of the field for about 30m and head diagonally right towards the left end of the greenhouses in the distance **(A)**. If the farmer has a crop in the field and you prefer not to cause any damage (although it would in theory be trespass) you can follow the track around the perimeter of the field and behind the row of greenhouses.

At the very corner of the field just beyond the end of the greenhouses, the ditch can be crossed easily in the middle of the copse of trees. Having crossed the ditch, turn left and follow its line around to the left and up the gently sloping side of the field to the hedgerow at the top **(B)** with Woodcock Farm to your left. Follow the hedge line around to the right and head for the far corner of the field. The Ordnance Survey map is incorrect here as one of the hedgerows coming up from the nurseries has been removed.

At the top corner of the field, go through a gap in the hedge, over a stile and across a small field to another hedge **(C)**. At the time of writing there was no stile in this hedge. The only way I can see of getting from one field to the other is by heading for the top corner of the field where the hedge is thinner and fighting your way through, even though this is 30m off course. Once into the next field, follow the original direction and the hedge line to the right, with the cream gable end of Low Woodcock over to your left. Again the field markings are not quite right, as a hedge running down from the farm has been ripped out. Carry on following the line of the hedge for approximately 400m. It is not clear which side of the hedge you are supposed to be on and I think the map draughtsman hedged his bets and ran the path on top of the hedge line for some way **(D)**.

At the first gate by the corner of the field turn right and immediately left, and proceed with the hedgerow now on your left. In the absence of any waymarked footpaths, you will need to be very

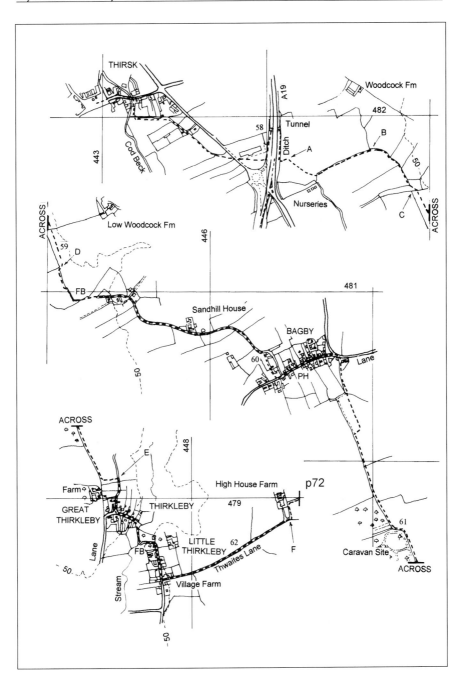

confident of your own map reading capabilities. Keep following the line of the hedge across a bridge and through a gate in the distance to – at last – the first waymarked sign for over a mile. Here, you can congratulate yourself on your map reading skills.

Follow the waymarked sign around the field, through a gate and down a track, and out on to the tarmac lane in front of Bagby Grange. The next few miles are easily walked and the pace may increase accordingly.

Follow the lane into Bagby. The church at Bagby is unusual for this area, with its central pyramid and spired roof, and what appears to be a fish as a weather vane. Follow the lane up onto the main road and turn left. I had originally intended going virtually straight across here but there is now a new house and the path goes through the front garden and across a field to the rear. Apparently, the farmer makes walkers most unwelcome. Pass the Greyhound Inn where food is available and follow the road to the top of the village passing some lovely brick houses on the left. Unfortunately, there has been a lot of new development in Bagby, which has not been built to match the colour or style of the original buildings.

At the end of the road, turn right and then right again (just before the small petrol station) on a waymarked bridleway now heading for Great Thirkleby. Turn right through the gate at the corner of the cricket field and, after 50m, turn left along the side of the hedge. For the next mile, the path follows the hedge line through to Great Thirkleby.

The first clear views can be seen of the White Horse of Kilburn just below Sutton Bank Airfield (extensively used for gliders) as you approach Great Thirkleby. Indeed on a sunny day a number of gliders should be seen from the path. Towards the end of the second-to-last field before the village, turn left towards the hedge. Cross the stile in the middle of the fence and follow the fence line down to the hedge, through a gate and on to the lane **(E)**.

Turn right into Great Thirkleby. At the end of the lane, pass the village hall on your right and turn left down the hill. This is a lovely little village with red brick houses, which seem to blend in perfectly with the surroundings. At the bottom of the hill, turn right and join the grass path, following the waymark sign with the stream to your left.

Cross the stream at the end of this path and head up the hill into Little Thirkleby, turn right at the top of the hill and follow the tarmac lane with the houses to your right. Three new houses have been built here so whether or not the term Little Thirkleby is still correct I do not know, as the new houses are equivalent in number to the original village size. At the next farm on your left (Village Farm), follow the waymarked footpath (Thwaites Lane), left. There is a good view of the White Horse of Kilburn, which is more grey than white. A new coat of paint would not go amiss – maybe it has had one by now! This Victorian creation was based on the ancient White Horse at Uffington, cut into chalk hills on the 'Ridgeway' near Swindon. Thomas Taylor formed the Kilburn horse in 1857 with 20 men and using six tons of lime wash. The horse is almost 100m long and 70m high.

As you approach High House Farm, you will note that the footpath has been officially diverted (**F**). Leave the tarmac road and walk forward on the grass in the same direction for about 30m. Then, turn left down the hedge line and right down the track (150m to the north and parallel to the route indicated on the Ordnance Survey map). The blue waymarks are few and far between.

At the bottom of the field the track crosses a hedge line, turn right just after the hedge following the waymarked track for 100m (see below for alternative route). Turn left just after a corner in the hedge following a bridleway across the field (in the original direction of Thwaites Lane). Head just to the right of Stockhill Farm in the distance, for over a mile (through six fields). In the field before Stockhill Farm, keep to the right fence through the gates. At the top right corner of the last field, turn left into the track via a gate. After 200m, turn right on the lane and into the centre of Kilburn

Kilburn is famous for two things: the white horse and Robert 'Mousey' Thompson. The Kilburn carpenter and cabinetmaker is world famous for his carvings of small mice on chair legs, benches, door corners etc. His first commission was at the small church at Hubberholme in the Yorkshire Dales. It is said that, when asked why he had carved the tiny animals, he stated that it was because he was, "as poor as a church mouse".

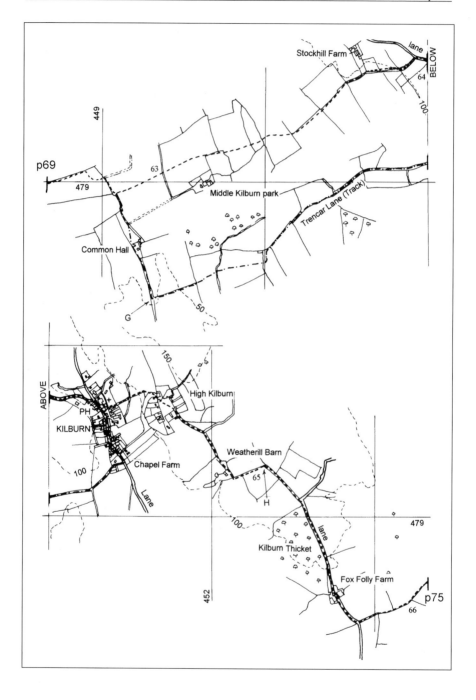

Examples of his work can be found in Otley Methodists church, Ripon Cathedral and the medieval chapel of St Thomas in St Mary's Kilburn.

Trencar Lane Alternative:

The chosen path across to Stockhill Farm was at one time impassable (now cleared thanks to the efforts of Hambleton Council) and the following route can be used as an alternative. Follow the track along the hedge line towards the farmhouse in the distance called Common Hall. The track turns into a tarmac lane (Common Lane). After a further 200m, look for the waymarked signs to your left at the end of the large field (G). This path, Trencar Lane, is well used and the route is obvious, following in the same general direction for about a mile. At the end of Trencar Lane, turn left into the lane and into Kilburn.

Kilburn is a lovely little village, quiet and sleepy, with traditional stone houses that are almost Cotswold-like in appearance. At the Foresters Arms Hotel, turn left into the yard and head for the top left corner of the square and into the church grounds. Take the path up to the right, passing a stone cross (made to look like wood!) and out of the church grounds via a white wooden kissing gate. Head up the hill towards High Kilburn, having passed through two further gates and across a track. At the top of the path, go through a gate and onto a small lane leading further up the hill. Stay on the lane through High Kilburn village and, where the lane turns sharply to the left, follow the waymarked sign straight on down to Weatherhill Barn.

Go through two gates and carry on the line of the track passing the stone barn and heading for the waymarked sign in the top left-hand corner of the paddock. Go through a gate and keep the wire fence to your left, walking up the hill to a stile in the top left-hand corner of the field. Enter an old tree lined track now very overgrown **(H)** and at the end turn right onto the lane, which is to be followed for the next half a mile. Two hundred metres after Fox Folly Farm, take the waymarked footpath to the left over a stile and into a field following the right hedgerow. Do not cross the footbridge to the right after 100m. After about half a mile, at the bottom of the field by a copse of trees, cross the footbridge and go over the stile proceeding up through the woods on the well marked footpath. At the top of the next field, turn right, picking up the footpath diversion around Camshead Farm waymarked to Byland Abbey. Just after joining this footpath, the first glimpses of Byland can be seen in the distance. Follow the well waymarked path to Byland Abbey just over half a mile ahead, eventually the path comes out onto the road..

Turn left onto the road passing the Abbey Inn, around the side of the abbey and after 400m with the abbey on your right turn left down a driveway (just after the millstone with the Byland Abbey sign on it).

Turn immediately right over a footpath diversion and across a further stile into the next field heading for the top corner towards the red tiled houses in the distance (now heading for Wass and the Cleveland escarpment). Pass through the kissing gate at the side of a bench and left toward the waymarked sign by the gate. Go over the stile and along the grass track to the gate in the next field.

Turn right down the lane and left in Wass by the Wombwell Arms, up Wass Bank Road signposted 'Helmsley via Wass Bank 1:6', passing the very small and charming church of St Thomas on the right with its external bell. This hill (approximately 160m) is the only real climb of the day. At the top of the hill as the road starts to flatten out you enter a conifer plantation with trees on both sides. Turn left and follow the waymarked public bridleway into the woods. After about 150m the main track bends away to the left, do not follow this but carry straight on between the trees. This path was used in the 12th and 13th centuries as a direct route between Byland and Rievaulx abbeys. It is interesting to think of the many monks and tradesmen following the same route as you are now, all those years ago without the assistance of waterproof leather walking boots and Gore-Tex clothing.

Keep following this general direction for half a mile until the main Thirsk / Helmsley Road is crossed.

The village of Old Byland can be seen across the valley. Cross the road, turn right and after 100m left down the waymarked farm track. It is unfortunate that Rievaulx Abbey cannot be seen from this vantage point, although the view over the North York Moors is fantastic.

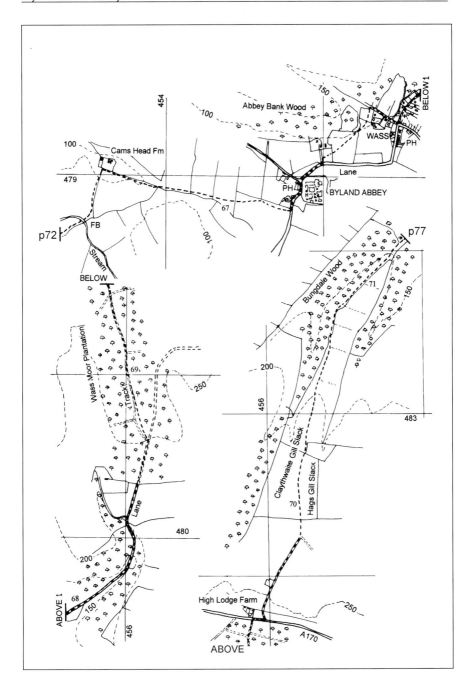

At the time of writing High Lodge Farm had quite a number of deer, a modern form of live stock for the farmers. Shortly after lambing, I had the pleasure of seeing a nanny goat suckling two lambs, and the lambs following the goat just as if she were their real mother. The route from High Lodge Farm is wonderful for walking with lovely grassy tracks leading slightly downhill. Carry straight on down the hill following the indentation of the old track. The line of the bridleway is some three to four feet below the adjacent land, clearly evidence of a great deal of use in bygone times.

Glimpses of Rievaulx Abbey can now be seen down in the valley to the right.

Having passed through a number of gates, the track drops down into the side of the wood **(J)**. This is known as Hags Wood a common name in Yorkshire with various meanings: soft place on a moor, a firm place in a bog, a witch and of course an ugly old woman. I am not sure how the name was derived but Abbot Hagg Farm near to Rievaulx Bridge was almost certainly taken from 'hagio' meaning 'of saints' or 'holy'.

Join a track coming in from the right and carry on downhill onto the small lane in the valley. Turn right onto the lane at the corner of Cross Green Farm and as the road splits keep to the right sign-posted Helmsley and Rievaulx, cross a bridge and turn left to Rievaulx Abbey (half a mile up the road).

Rievaulx Abbey really should not be missed – it is one of the best-preserved abbeys in Yorkshire.

Having visited Rievaulx, return to the bridge and carry on to Helmsley. After about half a mile (just after the road bends to the left) turn right on the waymarked path signposted 'Helmsley 2 miles'.

The path now follows the *Cleveland Way* with the remainder of the walk through to Helmsley well signposted. After just under a mile pass Griff Lodge, a folly with spectacular views overlooking the valley. Cross the track into woods. As the path leaves the woods the first view of Helmsley Castle can be seen a mile in front. The wide hard clay path you are now on is a tribute to the popularity of the *Cleveland Way*. Unfortunately, this is not good for the foot-weary

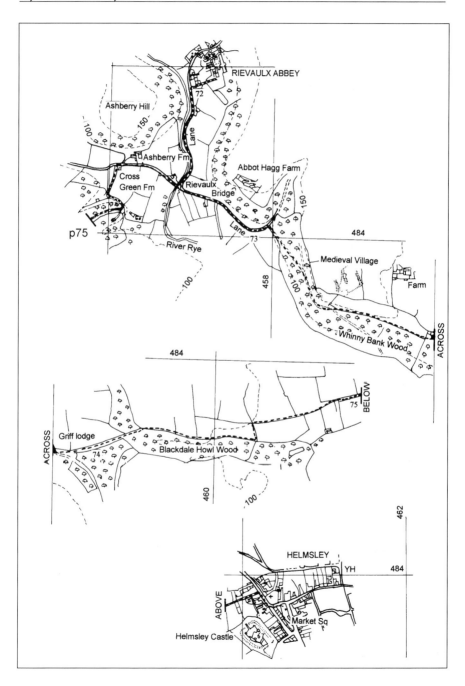

traveller who, at this stage of a long day's walk, would prefer a nice grassy path.

After a small distance the path turns sharp left and immediately turns right again down into Helmsley half a mile away. At the end of the lane, carry straight on and turn right down into Helmsley centre.

Byland Abbey

Byland is a Cistercian abbey and was constructed at the same time as Fountains and Rievaulx the three being called the Three Luminaries of the North. The monks who founded Byland came from the Savignac Abbey of Furness. Before arriving at Byland, they moved from Furness to Calder, near Egremont, on the west coast of Cumbria in 1134. The new monastery was raided by the Scots and the monks tried to return to Furness, but were thwarted. They had heard of the Archbishop Thurston of York, who had helped the community at Fountains Abbey, and decided to move in that direction.

However, at Thirsk they were befriended by Gundreder Gorbeny, who encouraged them to join a hermit at Hudd, east of Thirsk. The site at Hudd was too small, however, and with growing numbers they moved in 1143 to the site at Old Byland. This new site was less than two miles from Rievaulx and this lead to obvious friction (The bells and chanting from each mon-

Byland Abbey

astery could be heard by their respective neighbours at all hours). So in 1147 they moved again to Stocking. A small monastery was built here and the monastic community became Cistercian. Roger Mowbray who granted the land had also included an area of swampy land a mile and a half east of Stocking and the monks began clearing and draining it. The Cistercian community had grown considerably by this time. The new monastery at Byland was not considered habitable until 1177 some 30 years after having been granted the land and over 43 years since starting out on their original adventure.

Byland prospered and, by the year 1200, most of the buildings were complete. Byland was still prosperous 100 years later but it was pillaged by the Scots in 1322. Edward II was reputed to have been dinning at Byland just before the raid and was almost captured. When the abbey was surrendered to the Crown on the 30 November 1538, there were 25 monks in place. The church is again large, being 350ft (106m) long with an aisled nave of 11 bays. The west front is the greatest surviving feature of the abbey with its great wheel window 26ft (8m) in diameter. The floor of the church would have been tiled in a green and yellow pattern and, in certain areas, this tiling remains. After the Dissolution, the site was granted to Sir William Pickering. A dwelling house was constructed from part of the eastern range but little remains of the construction.

Rievaulx Abbey

Rievaulx was the first of a celebrated group of northern Cistercian foundations and takes its name from the site in the Rye Valley. The land was granted in 1131 by Walter L'espec, Lord of Helmsley, and was colonised directly by monks from Clairvaux in France, headed by the Abbot, William, an Englishman. The monks actually arrived in 1132 and the abbey grew at a phenomenal speed with the number of monks and lay brothers increasing to 300 within 10 years. In the period 1147-67 there were reputed to be 140 monks and 600 lay brothers and Rievaulx sent out monks to found new houses as Melrose, Warden, Dundrenen and Reversby. Ailred, who was Abbot from 1147 to 1167, was English by birth but had risen to become the steward of the household of the Scottish King David I.

Ailred was sent on a mission to see Archbishop Thurstan of York and, while there, received his calling to become a monk at Rievaulx Abbey. Ailred had a swift passage through the ranks to become the third Abbot in 1147 (he was 37 years old). His fame spread far and wide and he was a respected friend of King Henry II. He corresponded regularly with popes, kings, and bishops and also wrote a *Genealogy of the Kings of England* and *A Life of Edward the Confessor*. As Rievaulx established its spiritual reputation, there was a surge of building, which lasted over a century. However, the majestic buildings created a large debt and the abbey soon declined. By 1380, with the help of the Black Death, the number of monks had fallen to fifteen with three lay-brothers and, due to this, superfluous parts of the building were demolished in the 15th century. Dissolution arrived on the 3 December 1538 by which time 21 monks were left.

The church at Rievaulx is most unusual in that the axis of the building is 90° to the conventional way in which Cistercian abbeys are built. The site is steeply sloping and, therefore, the building could not be built on the normal east-west axis. The church itself was completed in the 13th century and is about 370ft (112m) in

Rievaulx Abbey

length. The large Nave is the oldest standing Nave of its size in France or Britain and is constructed in the severe Cistercian manner. The west tower arch has massive shafted piers, which are 75ft (23m) in height topped with short windows with pointed arches. After the Dissolution, the site was granted to Thomas Earl of Rutland who also owned the Helmsley Estates.

Helmsley

In the Market Square look for the ancient market cross in the corner of the spacious square. A stone canopy rises over the marble statue of William 2nd Baron Feversham; it was built in 1871 and dominates the market scene.

Walter L'Espec, who also founded Rievaulx and Kirkham abbeys, founded Helmsley castle. The earliest remaining masonry dates from the end of the 12th century when the keep, walls and towers were constructed during the time of Robert de Ros (1186-1227) who with his wife, Isabel, held it against King John's siege in 1216. The barbican, built to protect the gatehouse in the 13th century, is pierced with loopholes for longbowmen. The defensive arrangements are impressive – two lines of ditches surround the main fortifications.

The castle briefly belonged to King Richard III, 1478-1485. It was modified down the centuries, eventually becoming more of a residential mansion – the domestic buildings date from the 16th century and examples of Tudor woodwork and plasterwork can be seen.

The castle was besieged in 1644 by the Parliamentarians under Sir Thomas Fairfax, with 700 foot soldiers, 300 horsemen and cannon placed to the south. Sir Thomas was wounded on Rye Bank, but after three month's siege, Sir Gordon Crosland surrendered. The castle was rendered indefensible and later removal of stone by local people led to further decay. The domestic building remained in use until Duncombe Park mansion was completed around 1713 (about half a mile south west of the castle).

Inside the Parish Church are some interesting murals, which illustrate the history of the church and the parish.

The nearby Duncombe Park, family home of Lord and Lady Feversham, has an extensive historic parkland and National Nature

Reserve. Sir Charles Duncombe, wealthy banker and Lord Mayor of London, acquired Helmsley Castle in 1689. He was succeeded by his brother-in-law, Thomas Browne, who took the Duncombe name. The architect, William Wakefield, Squire of Huby Hall near Easingwold, designed the original Duncombe Park mansion.

Day 6: Helmsley To Rosedale Abbey

Distance: 16.5 miles

Map: Outdoor Leisure 26

Refreshments: Shop & Pubs at Gillamoor, Hutton-le-Hole cafés at Hutton-le-Hole, Pub at Lastingham

This is an interesting day's walk on the southern slopes of the North York Moors with steep-sided valleys, followed by a short moorland stretch before Rosedale Abbey. Food can be obtained at various cafés at Hutton-le-Hole and at the pub at Lastingham. There is a pub at Gillamoor, which serves excellent food but this may be a bit o.t.t. for a lunchtime (there is also a village shop). The museum at Hutton-le-Hole and especially the crypt at Lastingham are not to be missed no matter how short of time you are.

Head away from Helmsley on the main Pickering road and, after approximately 400m, follow the sign towards the youth hostel. Then, after 100m, head right on the waymarked track between houses. The path is well defined, leading towards Rea Garth Farm with splendid view of Helmsley and the castle behind. As you rise up the small hill, head for the gate to the right of the barns (in between the barns and the farmhouse). Through the farmyard and turn left on to Monk Gardens Lane leading northwards. As you approach the woods of Ricall Dale, keep following the track around the corner in the same general direction as before – do not drop down into the valley.

Old Rea Garth Farm, of which only the barns remain standing, is passed after 300m, the farmhouse being a pathetic ruin. Follow the high level track for just over half a mile before dropping down Low-Tun Way into Ricall Dale, just after entering the woods **(A)**.

A peculiarity of today's section of the walk is that the valleys in

Stone crusher in Helmsley

this area run north to south and the path heads generally in the direction west to east. Therefore, there is a bit of 'up and down' work to do. The valleys themselves are generally unpopulated and are superb for contemplative peaceful walking. As you approach the bottom of the valley keep left as a track comes in from the right. After a further 400m take the track diagonally down to the right towards the stream in the bottom. At the next junction keep left heading up the valley (do not cross over the river). The bottom of the valley is coated with a beautiful spread of wild flowers in summer with sweet bracken in between deciduous woodland.

Pass though the side of a gate, following the waymarked sign, into an area quite often used by Scouts in the summer – a more idyllic camping spot is hard to imagine. Head through the open area that is used for the camp and into the woods along a well-defined footpath, still heading up the valley and through a gate marked 'Bull'. Part of this route may be adopted for the Cleveland Way Link between Filey and Helmsley. Cross the valley/stream by way of the concrete footbridge and begin the ascent past Hasty Bank Farm back toward the barns and then up past the side of the farmhouse. The farmhouse, although very run down, would appear to be used for a holiday let. When I last walked this route there was a small hand-written sign outside saying 'Teas 30p' – you wish! **(B)** At the top of the track, turn right up the side of the valley (now heading south for a short while).

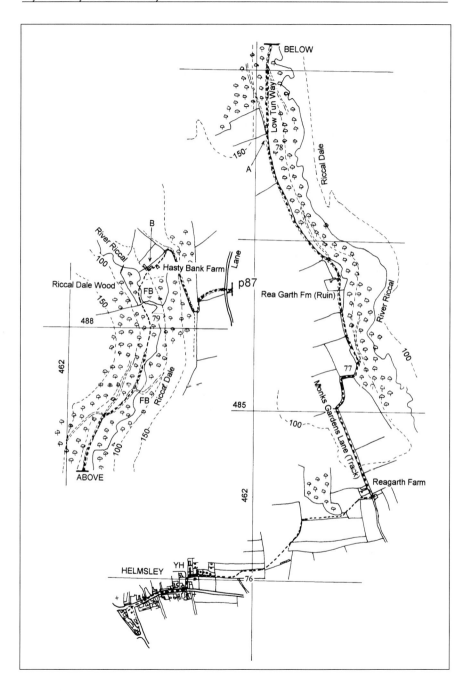

At the top of the hill, follow the track as it curves round to the left and back north for 50m through two gates and onto the road in the distance. Cross the road and through the gate on the other side noting that here is the post box, dustbin etc for Hasty Bank Farm, some walk to get rid of your rubbish and collect the mail! Follow the right hedge downhill, through a gate and carry on into the valley bottom, through another gate and up the other side. At the end of the next field, cross the road and carry on, heading in the same direction down towards the woods. There is a good view over to the right of the Vale of Pickering and York. Head down into the wood and immediately out the other side onto a tarmac road and follow the lane uphill – not on the private road – **(C)**.

You are now passing to the right of Norton Tower Plantations and Gardens with hopefully the heady perfume of flowers wafting across. I have not been to the gardens myself but I have been told that they are rather spectacular and very popular in spring and summer. Carry straight on the lane, now with views towards the coast and East Yorkshire in front, and Norton Tower back to the left. At the end of the lane turn left towards Wether Cote Farm, do not follow the 'link' sign. We are now again heading north. As the lane bends round to the farm, carry straight on through the gate and on the track. The field to the right has spectacular displays of buttercups and daisies in early summer. Now you have the first glimpses of the moors in the distance and Rudland Rigg.

Through the next gate, as the track forks, turn immediately right, down the fence line (do not follow either track), to the line of trees ignoring the small gate on the right. Pass a telegraph pole and on to a path leading downhill and to the left. At the bottom of the hill, take the gate leading downhill out of the woods, to a gate in the bottom right corner of the field **(D)**. Again, enjoy lovely views over the moors. Take the *second* gate and follow the track towards a farm. At the end of the field take the lower of the two gates (waymarked) and follow the track down to the farm entrance and cross a waymarked wall into the field at the side of the farm. Head across the field to a gate and then slightly down to a further gate toward the bottom of the next hedgerow.

Cross the stile and then the river footbridge in the bottom corner

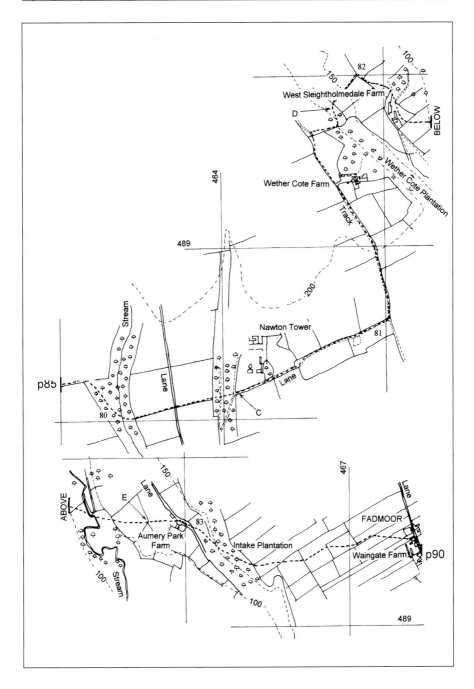

of the next field (a good spot for a picnic). The footpath here is rather unclear. A track does follow the river but do not follow this. Instead, head diagonally up the hill, in the same general direction as before. Make toward a patch of gorse bushes on a faint track between two large trees and into some more gorse bushes beyond. As long as you keep heading diagonally left you will see the waymarked stile in the top corner of the field just above a bank **(E)**.

Go over the stile and head diagonally across the next field towards the farm and to the gate in the right-hand corner below the old farm outbuildings. At the lane turn right along the side of Aumery Park Farm, an unspoilt Yorkshire farmhouse. Immediately after the farm, turn left up the hill along the waymarked footpath to the left of the electricity pylon. At the top of the hill, turn right and, after approximately 50m go left, over the stile. Then head diagonally across the field (the crops are sprayed off to indicate the line of the path, which is both helpful to walkers and prevents accidental damage).

Look for a stile approximately midway through the next hedge line and, for the following few fields, keep a close eye out for the waymarked stiles in the general direction of Fadmoor. Turn right into the lane and then left towards Gillamoor passing a house on the right with round windows and the Plough Inn in the far corner of the village. Fadmoor is a quiet little village with an open plan arrangement typical or many North Yorkshire villages. They have tried to build the few new houses 'in keeping' with the older ones but unfortunately they are rather too plain and have the wrong type of stone (preventing them from blending in exactly).

As you walk through Gillamoor passing the Royal Oak Inn, notice the sundial on the left, this is the grandest sundial I have seen (although it still does not appear to cope with British Summertime!).The sundial was erected by subscription in 1802 (although the date on the stonework is AD MDCCC) to celebrate the centenary. It was organised by the local schoolmaster J. Russell and has an elaborate system of four faces and twelve marked months to give an accurate time throughout the year. Carry on through the village down to the church and bear right at the cenotaph and down a path to the right of the church between the church and a house. The church at Gillamoor is simple and without embellishment (a good thing).

There is still a working communal water hydrant in Gillamoor, which is very unusual as most of these hydrants have gone into disrepair. At the bottom of the path turn sharp right back on the 'Link' footpath and follow the track down to Mill House. Take the diverted path round the left-hand side and cross an old millrace. A circular hole can be seen in the old stone wall, which would have housed the waterwheel shaft.

Cross the stream by way of the footbridge and head uphill following the right hedge line and crossing a stile at the top into the adjacent field. Head across the next field to a large tree in the fence line, to the left of two small overhead power poles. Walk in the same direction to the top right-hand corner of the next field joining a line of trees **(F)**.

Over a footbridge, turn left onto the track and immediately right on a grassy footpath running parallel with the stream, heading up onto the grassy path on the top of the embankment. After approximately 100m, the path splits into two, the main branch up toward the house on the hill-top and one going off towards the right. Take

Hutton-le-Hole

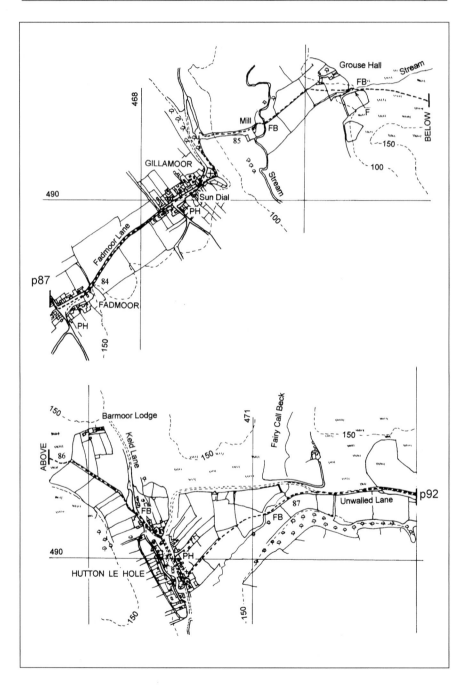

the right-hand fork heading toward the dip on the horizon. Follow the springy path for approximately 300m, looking for a waymarked fenced footpath heading down toward Hutton-le-Hole. The path leads into a small farm lane at which point turn right across the field to the adjacent stile and follow the fence line down to a gate leading into the road. Turn right and head down into the centre of Hutton-le-Hole, a very popular and pretty village with pubs, cafés and the famous folk museum.

Through Hutton-le-Hole, pass the folk museum and, just after St Chad's Church, take the waymarked footpath to the left – leading up behind a small house and to the side of the church into a field. Follow the left-hand fence line towards the waymark at the top of the field, you will see the thatched roofs of the folk museum over to the left.

At the end of the fourth field, cross the footbridge into the woods. Go out onto the road and turn right. As the road starts to dip down just before the junction with the road from Spaunton, there is a place on the map called the Mary Magdalene Well. I have looked for this a few times but without success. There is also an obvious short cut on the map to avoid Lastingham but Lastingham is a *must* visit, with the Crypt at St Mary's Abbey Church and lots of beautiful old buildings.

The Crypt, built in 1078 on the site of a Celtic monastery, is unspoilt as yet by tourism. As you enter, especially if you are alone, it is like being whisked back in time to the 11th century – an experience not to be missed.

Turn left at the junction, still heading for Lastingham. Note the row of cottages on the right with the very low eaves and dormer windows (typical of Yorkshiremen to cram a quart into a pint pot!) and, after half a mile, walk into the centre of Lastingham. Pass between the church on the right and the Blacksmith Arms, then turn left through the village, past the shrine of St Cedd (the founder) on the left and left again. Walk steadily uphill and across the moor towards Lastingham Ridge and Rosedale Abbey. Notice the shrine of St Chad on the right (St Cedd's brother).

There is now a steady climb up to a height of approximately 1,000ft (330m). Follow the wide waymarked track marked Rosedale Abbey (at the side of the fence) for the next mile and a half always go-

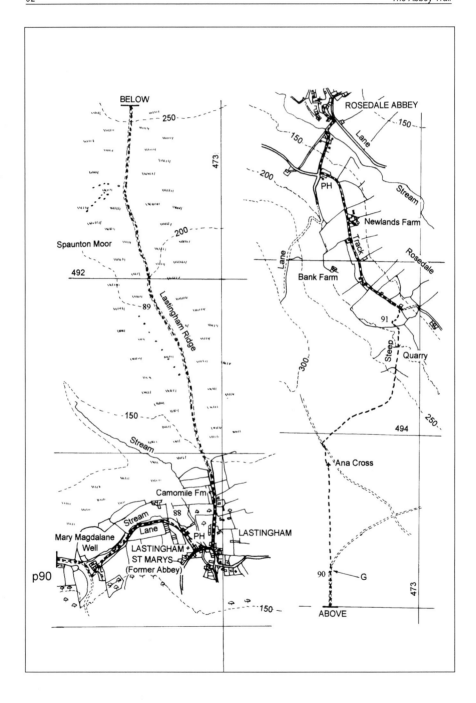

ing towards the top of the hill. Just before the top, take a small path leading off to the left towards a cross **(G)**.

The cross is a good point to have a breather and take in the panoramic views with the first view down Rosedale.

From the cross head straight on down onto the main path and then after 50m bear right on the waymarked path heading down towards Rosedale Abbey but *not* on the main path. This is not a well-used path and can be easily missed. The path leads down to a waymarked sign at the top of the cliff. The descent down to the valley bottom is quite steep and can be treacherous in winter. Take your time and take care, this descent is another test of your walking poles.

At the bottom of the hill, turn left and cross the stream, noticing the bright orange residue from iron ore. Proceed around the fence line to the gate on the opposite side of the quarry. Through the gate and after about 25 m turn right down the track leading to the gate at the bottom. Turn left onto the farm track shortly passing two rather grand houses on the left. The next house on the right is known as Newlands Farm – funnily enough, the same name as my old house in Tong. Unfortunately, the fine Georgian house is in a poor state of repair with severe corrosion from acids around the chimneys. Walking down the lane, the valley seen immediately in front is North Dale the start of tomorrow's walk. At the end of the track by the White Horse Farm Hotel, turn right down the main road into Rosedale Abbey, and at the end of the road turn left and up into the centre of the village.

St Mary's Abbey Church, Lastingham

A monastery was founded on this site in AD 654 by St Cedd, one of six brothers trained at Lindisfarne. The brothers Cedd, Cynebil, Caelin and Chad are mentioned in the *History of The English Church and People* written by the venerable Bede in 731. In AD 635, Cedd and his brothers were chosen by King Oswald of Northumbria to be trained by St Aidan as monks and missionaries. St Aidan came from the famous monastery in Iona in Scotland and became Bishop to King Oswald.

Cedd died from the plague in AD664 and the abbacy was bequeathed to his brother Chad. St Chad did not stay at Lastingham for long. Cedd's wooden 'church' was eventually replaced by a stone structure, some of the stones of which can by seen in the crypt. The monastery suffered greatly from the Viking invasions of the 9th and 10th centuries and went into decline. In 1078 the abbot of Whitby. Stephen obtained permission from William the Conqueror to re-build the monastery at Lastingham. The crypt was built as a shrine to St Cedd over the location where he was buried. The abbey church was constructed above the crypt but the abbey was never completed. It was abandoned in 1088 when Stephen moved to York and established the abbey of the same name (St Mary's). As you walk through the village, a shrine to St Cedd is seen on the left.

The inscription reads as follows

CEDD

ABBIE LASTING AE FVNDATOR

AD 654

OBITT AD664 ET SEPVLTVS EST

IN ECCLESIA A DEXTRA ALTARIS

The rough translation of which is 'Cedd the founder of Lastingham Abbey in AD654 died AD664 and was put in a grave in the church on the right of the altar'.

St Cedd founded three monasteries, with Lastingham being the best-known. It was said that the spot where the church was built was given by King Ethelwald and that Cedd spent forty days in prayer and fasting at this spot. Cedd was present at the famous synod of Whitby and wished to retain the Irish date for Easter but accepted the synod decision to stay with the Roman date as we have now . Shortly after his return to Lastingham, Cedd died of the plague and, on hearing the news, 30 monks came from London to spend their lives where the founder died. Unfortunately, they too caught the plague and were buried near the chapel. Cedd was also the second bishop of the City of London. St Chad (Ceadda) stayed at Lastingham until 669, when he was called to become the Bishop of the Mercians and went on to establish a monastery at Lichfield

Rosedale Abbey (Priory)

Rosedale grew around the abbey with industries such as iron foundering, tanning and sheep farming. Farmers sold cattle, oxen, butter and timber as far away as Seamer Market near Scarborough. Coal was also mined in the area. The French developed a glass industry in the valley in the late 16th century and limestone was mined in quarries in the late 19th century. However, the main industry was iron with haul roads, railways and buildings covering the whole of the edge of the Rosedale Valley. One mine alone was mining up to 800 tonnes (800,000kg) daily. The mines started to close in 1885 with one mine continuing to 1911. Rosedale is now a small, quiet village the numbers only increased by tourists in the summer months.

Site of Rosedale Abbey (priory)

Turges Brundos of Liddell obtained Rosedale from King Henry I in 1121 to 1130. His son and daughter in law founded the Priory at Rosedale before 1157. The nuns had money and discipline problems, but they did have patrons who kept the prioress and nine nuns until the Dissolution. The building was raided by the Scots in 1322. A number of buildings survived until the mid-19th century. Very little remains of the priory buildings at this day. Sir Thomas Williamson at the priory in 1569 had 18 houses in the Vale, a cornmill, a bake house, a tannery, an old hermitage and a cottage at Battle Bridge Hill. The abbey foresters provided wood to smelt iron, indeed the nunnery itself was reputed to have an iron forge and tannery. Sheep's wool was sold from the common at the Great Road that ran up the east moor.

Day 7. Rosedale Abbey to Grosmont

Distance: 15.0m

Map: Outdoor Leisure 26/27

Refreshments: None

This is a shorter day's walk along the side of Rosedale, followed by a moorland section over the watershed between the southern North York Moors and Eskdale. The descent is via the delightfully named Great Fryup Dale. Contrary to the name there is no where to eat except towards the end of the walk at the village store and pubs of Glaisdale and the small café at Glaisdale Station. Although I have ended this day's walk at Grosmont, it has very little of architectural interest to commend it other than the main station for the North York Moors Railway. If you do not mind a slightly longer walk on this last day, Glaisdale or the Postgate inn at Egton Bridge may be better suited.

From the centre of Rosedale Abbey, take the Egton road , with the Milburn Arms on your left, passing two large yew trees by the side of the front entrance. Turn left along the waymarked footpath into the village hall car park. Go through this to a field, heading for a waymarked stile in the far corner and follow the path up the valley of Northdale, along the side of Northdale Beck, for half a mile. Cross two ladder stiles, then continue in the direction of the beck at a waymark post that is funnily enough sign-posted 'Waymark'.

Cross the ladder stiles, ignoring the old bridge on your left. After a further 100m, cross the footbridge and take the blue waymarked arrow to the right leading gently uphill (not the steep path to the left). Now head for a waymark sign where the path crosses the farm track, still heading steeply uphill and towards the ladder stile in the distance. There is a fine view up Northdale to your right.

Follow the path and track eventually passing the site of an old spoil heap and some outbuildings on the right, with what would appear to be a walled garden but no signs of a house **(A)**.

Take the track leading to the access lane to West Northdale Farm and then left still heading uphill. After about 50m, turn right through a gate onto the road and then immediately left through another gate down into a conifer plantation. You are following the old mine railway which, at one point, must have gone through a tunnel under the road. The next two miles of the walk are by means of the old mine railway line . It is interesting to note how a lot of areas that have been mined in the 17th and 18th centuries are now green open areas effectively preserved by their industrialisation. This is especially true in urban areas where this sort of land was felt not fit for development and has resulted in open areas for recreation and pleasure .

Follow the line of the track through conifer woodland. This railway was constructed completely by hand with no mechanical excavators or JCBs. The amount of labour needed must have been vast and I would imagine the working conditions in winter must have bordered on the impossible. This flat section of path is a reward for that early morning climb. Just after the curve in the railway bed, the waymarked path drops down through Clough House. After approximately 300m, it leads back up to the level of the track. If, however, you stay on the embankment you eventually join the open track again a little further on. This just saves dropping down 20 metres or so, but the path can be a little obscure in places. If you prefer to follow the waymarked footpath drop down through Clough House and on to the farm track following the farm track to the end, turning right back up the hill towards the railway path **(B)**.

After 500m, enter the open railway path with an old railway building on your left and partially demolished buildings in front of you. Take the track way past the buildings heading north. If you look closely, the majority of the land in this area has been worked at some time. At the far side of the valley there are so many quarries, shafts, borrow holes etc, that they are hard to count. As you come round the corner, just after the buildings, there is a wonderful view of Rosedale. (For anybody on a day trip to Rosedale, there is a smashing cir-

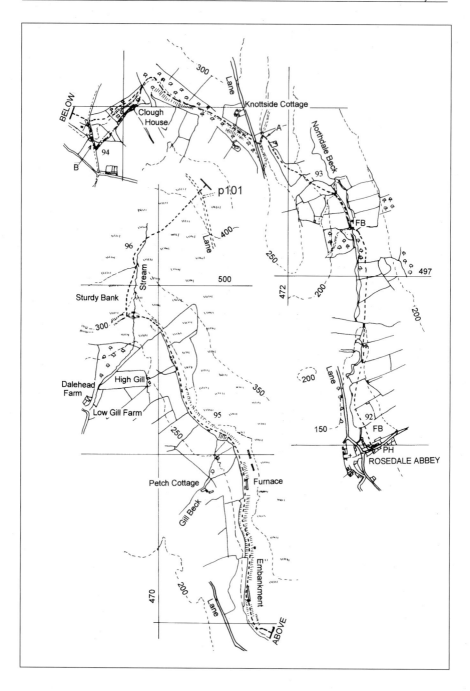

cular route following this path on towards Sturdy Bank, then turning left down through Dalehead Farm and on to Daleside Road all the way back to Rosedale Abbey via Forgill Farm, see separate day walk). Note the large mine workings to the right with huge blocks of carved sandstone forming the base to the arches, all of which would have been man-handled into position using rope block and tackle and shear hard graft.

The line of this railway once lead all round Rosedale to the head of Bank Top above Rosedale Abbey. It joined another railway from Farndale at Blakey Junction, adjacent to the road down to Churchhouses. Ironstone was extensively mined in this area. The next structure along is constructed using massive retaining walls, the last section has its original brick fire lining and the stonework is red and burnt, it was used as a furnace with the iron stone loaded from above and the fuel installed from below. Looking at the landscape as it is, it is hard to imagine where the fuel came from to fire the load.

As you come round the next bend in the railway bed, our route leads up to the right and can be seen to the far side of the sharp river valley. Immediately below is a plantation of trees and below that a collection of farm vehicles at Dalehead Farm. Cross the valley by way of a very sharply pointed embankment (obviously severely eroded) and at the end turn right heading up away from the railway.

There are two footpaths leading out of this valley. You must take the right-hand path, which keeps close to a stream. Indeed when it rains it is hard to distinguish between the stream and the path. Follow the line of pegs uphill having crossed the stream at one point and if in doubt follow the line of the stream. There is also one stone post and a small cairn acting as a waymark. Head up towards the road to another stone post marked 'Rosedale Whitby', the waymark sign pointing towards George Gap Causeway and Great Fryup Dale beyond.

Cross the road and carry on in the same direction enjoying the vast moorland view to the right . You are now at a height of 1350ft (410m) the highest point on the Abbey Trail **(C)**. Walking this section of path gives a great feeling of isolation. The stone trod, George Gap Causeway, was built for the miners and is still in reasonable condition. On examining some of the stones it is obvious that this path has been well used, with the stones being dished in the middle through continuous use. After 400m you will cross the line of the County Parish border at a causeway stone.

Proceed in the same direction, with the first view of Eskdale and the sea in the distance. At one point the stone trod disappears and leaves the track very wet and boggy. Proceed down the remnants of the stone trod coming out onto *Cut Road* the path used by the Coast to Coast route, turning right on the path for about 60m. At a cairn turn left down the hill, (noting the yellow spot on a stone at the side of the path) head steeply downhill, past waterfalls following the winding path to an area of old mine workings, eventually crossing a stream in the bottom, a great spot for a bite of lunch **(D)**.

Follow the waymark spots leaving the field by a gate taking the level path and slightly to the left. After 400m cross the stile on the right and head down the gully towards the now disused Dalehead Farm.

Take the track to the left side of the barns, through the gate and follow the farm track. The farm track crosses the stream and enters a tarmac lane with a strange-looking house (Fryup Lodge) to the left with ugly black windows and brown door. It is built from expensive ashlar stone, a very odd choice of material in this area. Even the barns are constructed of well cut virtually ashlar stone blocks. The route down Fryup Dale is generally by means of small country roads which are very rarely used, so the walking – although possibly hard underfoot – can be pleasant with no need to watch footing etc (a good time for a 'chin wag').

At Applegarth Farm (the first farm you come to after the lodge), where the road turns sharp right, carry straight on down the farm track with a wall to your left and a barn to your right with three infilled arches in its gable end. After a few metres the track splits into two, take the right-hand fork into the field with a 'bull' sign on the gate. Go through the left of the next two gates adjacent to a stile.

Follow the track through the gate at the end of the next field turning left to a gate approximately 50m away and head down to the waymark post in the corner of the field and onto a lane. Turn right and go through the tiny village of Street, and just after the last house

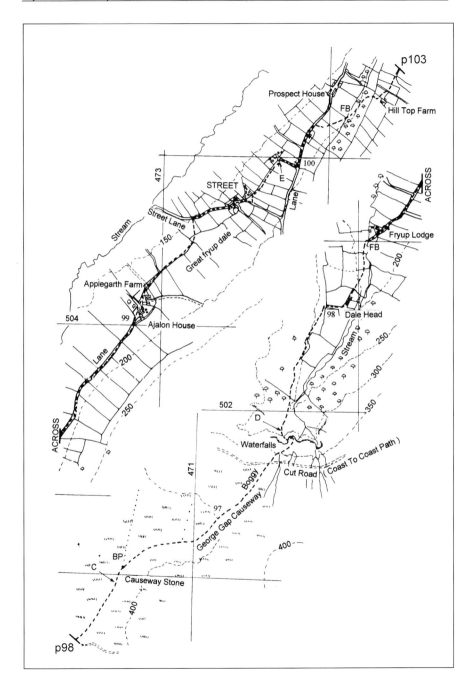

(High Farmhouse) turn left at the waymark sign into the drive for about 40m. Leave the drive by means of the gate and head for a series of stiles in the next few fields. Follow the wall line and leave the last field by means of the gate in the left-hand corner **(E)**.

Turn right up the tarmac track to the church, (I should say what was a church and is now a house) and turn left down the lane.

If you have time, a small diversion to view the Georgian windows of Prospect House may be worthwhile, 300m further down the lane towards Lealholm. At the time of writing, the building was unusual in that it still had its original Georgian glass and frames. As you can see looking from the side, the glass is not flat by any means but has dimples and depressions – clearly a sign of age and, more importantly, of being hand-made. This is also a testament to the quality of the old timber frames. It is easy to forget in these days of large sheet glass panels that the reason for the small Georgian windows was that glass was very expensive to make in big panes.

After approximately 200m pass a small post box on the left and turn right over a ladder stile through a small builder's yard and into a field, heading left going slightly uphill looking for a stile at the mid point in the wall. Cross the stile and head for the top corner of the next field behind gorse bushes leaving the field by way of the gate and follow the footpath up through the woods. On leaving the wood, head for the gate in the wall leading up towards Hill Top Farm.

Just before the farm, take the ladder stile to the left, crossing a small field and taking the stile heading for Shaw End Farm in the distance. Follow the same general direction towards the farm across a step stile into the next field and then turn right over another step stile by the side of the gate just before the farm and up onto the farm access road. Exit the farm access via a small gate by the side of the cattle grid and turn immediately left by the side of the wall and follow the wall line. As you approach double gates on the left, look for two waymarked posts on the right and turn right up onto the road **(F)**.

Turn left onto the road and opposite the next farm, ignoring the first waymark post. Make your way down to Busco Beck Farm – not a well-used path. The alternative is to walk down the road for a short while and turn right up the road at the 'T' junction. At Busco Beck

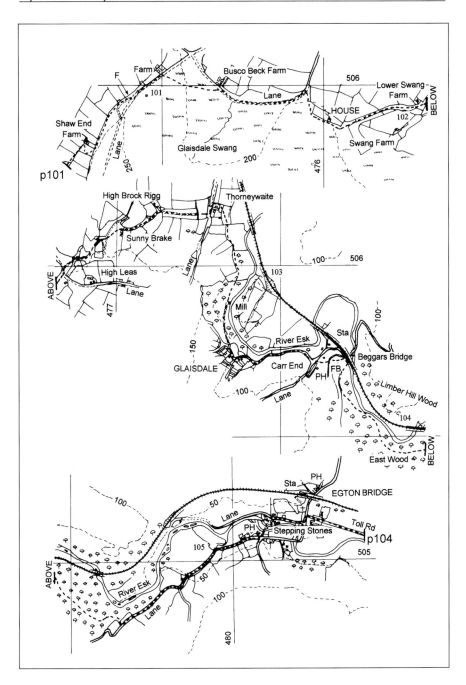

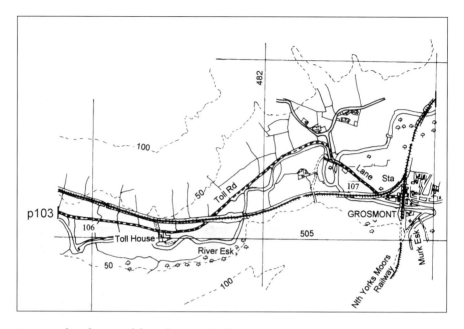

Farm take the road heading uphill, ignoring a waymark sign on the right. 100m after the brow of the hill turn right following the waymarked footpath by the side of the wall on the track round to a house. Leaving the gravel track and house behind, turn slightly left after the paddock and head for the gate just after beehives.

Leave the bottom of the long strip field by way of a gate and enter the farm track of Lower Swang Farm and out onto the road. Turn left and then immediately right down a further tarmac track past two houses in the bottom . Just after a bungalow you meet a track coming down from the right, head *straight across* onto a grass track between the bracken (do not take the gravel track to the left). Go through the gate at the bottom of the hill and follow the tree-lined track gently curving to the left and then the stone trod past the side of High Brock Rigg. Turn right onto a tarmac lane leading down to Thorneywaite. As you enter the road turn left and then right down through a beautiful garden (waymarked Glaisdale).

Follow the waymarked footpath into the woods, crossing a ladder stile, now hearing the rushing of the River Esk below. You have now joined the route of the Esk Valley Walk (the dolphin sign). Pass the

Beggar's Bridge

mill building with its old mill race and rusty remains of the original water wheel. It would be rather nice to see it restored and working. Proceed along the track leading steadily uphill coming through a kissing gate onto a lane. For anyone wishing to get refreshments there is a post office and pub at Glaisdale, if you are however pressing on to Egton Bridge turn left down the hill and along the lane by the side of the River Esk. At the end of the lane go straight across the road (at the left gable of the Arncliffe Arms) and go down the path to a footbridge in the bottom. The Arncliffe Arms, at the time of writing, served lunchtime and evening meals. Keep left at the side of the two houses and follow a track to a ford, over the footbridge and on to Beggars Bridge.

This packhorse bridge dated 1619 and initialled T F (Tom Ferris) is a wonderful example of this type of construction. The bridge is probably older than the date stone and may have been restored by Tom in 1619. Retrace your steps back under the railway arch and across the footbridge but now head up a line of earth steps leading up into the woods. The path follows the river for a few metres then eventually leads up a trodden path through the wood for about a mile.

At the top of the wood turn left down the road towards Egton. At the Horseshoe Hotel with its two enormous Scots pines in the grounds, turn left (before the main road) and take the footpath down to the stepping stones. When the river is in spate you will have to use the main road-bridge to cross the river. At the end of the stepping stones turn right over the mill race and pass between the old mill and a house in the corner. Turn right to the end of the lane, passing on the left a wonderful formal garden with rhododendrons, Scots pines and multitudinous flowers.

Egton Bridge is a small village with two pubs and no shops. Accommodation should not prove too difficult, although those who require supplies would have to collect them from either Glaisdale or Grosmont.

From Egton Bridge head north towards Egton and, after about 50m turn right down a waymarked route for Grosmont following the route for the Esk Valley Walk. This section of easy walking is also used by the Coast to Coast route. Roughly half way along this former toll road are the toll prices, motorcar one shilling, hearse six pence and various others. It seems a curious place to put the toll cottage in the middle of the toll road and not at either end. However, I suppose once you are on the road rather than turn back you would pay the fee and you need only pay one attendant of course.

Listen for the whistles from the North Yorkshire Moors Railway trains, which can often be heard on this section of the route. Eventually the toll road comes out on to a lane where, if you are stopping or need provisions, you turn right into Grosmont. At this point the Coast to Coast walkers head south for Robin Hoods Bay.

Day 8. Grosmont To Whitby

Distance: 9.0 miles

Map: Outdoor Leisure 27

Refreshments: Shops at Sleights & Sneaton

This is the final and shortest day's walk. I have tried to make this section as short as possible to allow time to visit Whitby or perhaps have enough time to travel home the same day. Most of the walk is along the Esk Valley with a small section towards the end overlooking Whitby and the abbey. Food shouldn't be a problem however there is a well-stocked shop at Sneaton and also a village pub.

Trace your steps back from Grosmont and turn right following the waymark sign for 'Sleights 3½ miles' and then turn right along the road aptly named (leading to) Priory Park. After 400m the road turns sharp left. Follow the Esk Valley Walk 'dolphin sign' straight along a farm track. Carry straight on to Grosmont Farm, go through the farm and along the track, heading steadily uphill. Cross a footbridge by a ford and head towards Fotherly's Farm up a steep track with a stone trod in the centre. Just before the farm gate turn left again following the Esk Valley Walk sign.

As the path splits keep right to the top of the hill. Follow the right-hand hedge line to the far corner of the field and then turn left for 50m. Follow the waymark signs through a gate and into the hedged stone path and out on to a farm lane past Newbiggin Hall. Carry straight on through two fields and into the woods via a small gate.

Leave the woods by a further small gate and into a field at the edge of the escarpment (do not take the gate going to the right downhill.) Follow the hedge on a stone trod. This stone trod is almost two miles long and is a feat of engineering in its own right, the cutting of the stone the transport and placing etc must have been a mammoth task.

Through three gates following the waymark signs down a clay

North York Moors Railway at Grosmont

bank which is also used by horses. At this point the stone trod has disappeared. At the bottom of the hill turn right on to a tarmac track and then left following a bridleway **(A)**. This is a slight diversion from the route of the OS map. After 40m turn left across the footbridge and up the hill at the other side. Follow the stone trod leaving the field by a stile onto a tarmac lane. Turn right and follow the lane to Thistle Grove (a collection of houses and a farm), and turn right again immediately before the houses on the waymark path, once again picking up the stone trod. At the top of the third field leave by means of a small gate and turn right down the tarmac track past Woodland Nursing Home and heading steadily downhill to Sleights. At the end of the lane carry straight on across the busy main road and on to the right-hand pavement at the side of the Esk. After 200m turn right over the footbridge to Sleights Station. Crossing this railway line is less daunting than that of the East Coast main line.

Cross the railway and head along Lowdale Lane, following the public bridleway between houses for 200m. Turn right heading slightly uphill for approximately 50m and then left along the public footpath. After 150m turn left over the footbridge (do not go straight

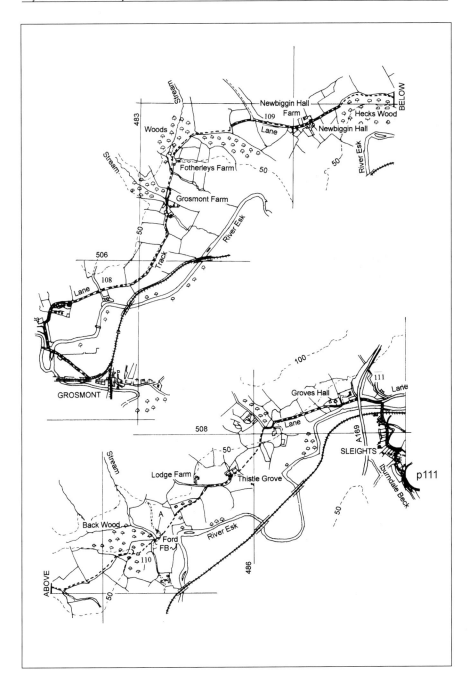

on). At the end of the track turn left following the waymark footpath signs around the back left of Berry Wood Farm complex and stables **(B)**.

Follow the fence line to the right crossing a footbridge on the right after 100m. From the footbridge head slightly to the left of the pylon and basically for the highest point in front of you (unfortunately) which eventually leads to a stile in the top corner of the field and into a small wood. The path comes out into a field with the church and village of Ugglebarnby in front. Follow the right hedge line for 200m and the stiles into the road and up to Ugglebarnby. Ugglebarnby must be near the top of the list of the most unusual village names in England. Ignore the sign for Sneaton and Whitby and carry on up the hill and left down the waymarked bridleway just before the end of the village.

After 50m ignoring the bridleway to the left, carry straight on the footpath up the steps. Through a stile into a field, head straight across the field in the same direction to a stile and on to the lane, now with a great view over Whitby and the sea. Turn right into the lane at which point you have a first view of Whitby Abbey standing majestically on the high ground above the old village, with the current church just below and the Youth Hostel in between. Where the road turns sharp left, carry straight on over the waymarked ladder stile and downhill into the little valley. Go across the footbridge and out via the slippery trod at the other side, nicely covered in light green moss to catch out the unsuspecting traveller. At the top of the little valley keep in the same direction (parallel with the left hedge line and approximately 150m from it) and head for the gate immediately in front of you, noting that the O.S. map is wrong here as yet a further hedge has been grubbed out. Take the path slightly left of Manor House Farm buildings to a stile in the fence and then through a few further stiles through to the main road and Sneaton. Cross the main road into Beacon Way towards the centre of Sneaton.

Refreshments can be obtained at the post office at Sneaton. The pathway down to the village church is quite interesting with a wonderful view over Whitby being obtained from the back of the church. Steps on the right-hand side of the entrance to the church were used for mounting horses. Two hundred metres after the church turn left

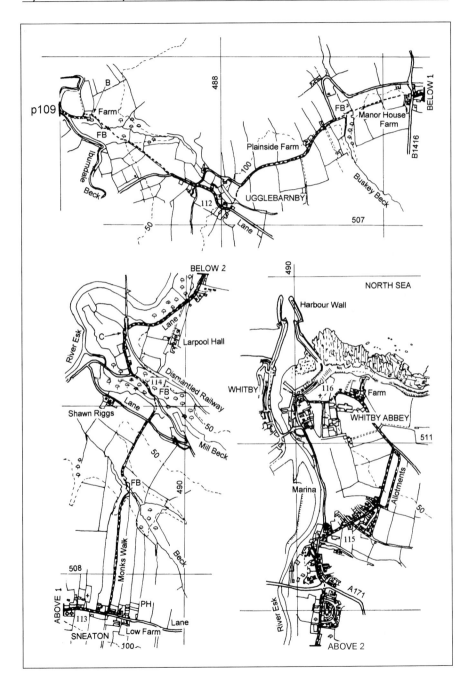

following the footpath to Whitby down the side of the aptly named 'Monks Farm', down Monks Walk at the side of a campsite on to yet another stone trod, the order of the day!

At the very bottom of the hill, cross the stream by means of a clapper bridge, following the trod up the hill and down the other side for 400m. Cross the lane and continue on the stone trod down into the woods. Go over the footbridge and turn left, now heading uphill through the woods. At the lane turn right heading uphill eventually passing underneath the old railway track **(C)**.

Although the track southward has been developed for bikes and walkers, the huge railway viaduct to the left is still closed – perhaps it will provide a spectacular way into 'new' Whitby in future. Follow this road for a further 500m, now entering the suburbs of Whitby with the abbey a short distance in front. Carry straight on across the main road and down Church Street. Bear left by the first red brick house (the old road leads slightly away from the main road), crossing the old road bridge. The walled inlet to the right may have been used as a dry dock . Note the splendid array of boats moored in the estuary. Turn left back on to the main road towards Whitby.

Turn right up Green Lane and, after 200m, take the waymarked path to the right. After 100m, turn sharp left along the lane behind houses and back onto Green Lane. Green Lane can get quite busy in summer – so here you can either walk up the lane to the junction or, after 10m, turn right onto the path through the allotments which eventually comes out just below the junction. At the junction, turn left on the flagged path and down to the abbey.

Congratulations – you have completed the Abbey Trail.

If you like peace and quiet, try to avoid Whitby on Bank Holidays as it can be spoilt by the large number of tourists. Having visited the abbey, you may wish to carry on down the famous stairs and, at the bottom, carry straight on down further stairs onto the quiet beach in Whitby harbour.

I hope you have enjoyed walking the Abbey Trail and visiting the ancient buildings as much as I did – and that it gave you a flavour of Yorkshire countryside and hospitality.

Whitby Abbey

Whitby Abbey affords a spectacular site on the summit of the east cliff very close to the centre of Whitby. The Benedictine abbey has a long history, with a religious house being founded in 657 by King Oswy of Northumbria. The king was celebrating his victory over the heathen King Pender of Mercia; he vowed that he would found twelve monasteries on the basis of his victory. Whitby was already a famous meeting place for the synod and this marked a new phase in British Christianity. Whitby figures prominently in *Bede's* history.

The settlement was destroyed in 867 by the Danes and the destruction was said to be so complete that nothing even of its foundations are known to remain The monastery was re-established by three monks from Gloucestershire. The site was given to them by the Northern Baron William Percy. However, the monks fell out with the founder and were later helped by William's brother who, in turn, improved relationships with William. Indeed the founder's son eventually became an Abbot. Reinfrid, a monk from Evesham, was appointed the Prior of the newly built foundation. William the Conquer himself granted the monastery a Charter of Privileges and these were extended by Henry I, in whose reign the Priory was raised to the status of abbey in the first decade of the 12th century. It was soon the third wealthiest Benedictine house in Yorkshire.

Although the Vikings plundered Whitby in 1153, the abbey does not seem to have suffered greatly. By the late 12th century, there were still 40 monks at Whitby. Building continued in the 13th and 14th centuries, financed in part by the successful revival of St Hilda's cult and Whitby became a mitred abbey. By the end of the 14th century however the numbers had dwindled and there were only 20 monks left. At Dissolution on the 14 December 1539 there were 22 monks left.

The net income at the time of the Dissolution was £437. At the Dissolution the roofs were removed but most of the walls stood until 1763 when the western side of the monastery was blown down. In 1830, the remains of the central tower collapsed and nine years later a large part of the choir also fell down.

The battered remains of the abbey reputedly received several direct hits from German cruisers shelling the north-eastern ports in

Whitby Abbey

1914. The church was built in the 13th century, completed in the 14th, and is over 300ft (100m) in length. The north wall of the north transept survives to its full height and has three tiers of lancet windows topped by a rose window gable. This is the dominant feature of the ruins, a very elaborate construction by Cistercian standards. The Benedictine monks have a more liberal attitude to the construction. In 1924, archaeological excavations revealed several remains of the Anglo-Saxon monastery.

Whitby

Where the River Esk reaches the North Sea, after crossing the uplands of North Yorkshire, the ancient seaport and the modern holiday resort of Whitby has grown to a town of some 14,000+ inhabitants. The east side, with its narrow winding streets and fishermen's cottages surmounted by the abbey, is perhaps more steeped in history than the relatively modern west side. The town is rightly proud of its association with famous men and its close and continuing links with the sea. Such industries as whaling, shipbuilding, sail making and rope making, all brought much prosperity to Whitby in their heyday.

A tradition of Whitby is the Planting of the Penny Hedge. The ceremony takes place yearly on the morning of Ascension Eve, at approximately 9 o'clock, and dates from 1159. It is said that Norman noblemen killed a hermit who had given sanctuary to a wounded wild boar they were hunting. Dying, the hermit was said to have forgiven them but the Abbot of Whitby ordered that, as a penance, they should erect a hedge every year on the mound of Whitby harbour, using a penny knife, or forfeit their lands. Since then, the penance has been faithfully carried out. This is but one of many interesting incidents in Whitby's history. Whitby held the famous 'Synod of Whitby'. It was in Whitby that monks representing the Celtic church and those accepting the rule of Rome, met in 664 AD to discuss variations in church custom and practice, notably methods of fixing the date of Easter. The system they agreed upon is the one in use today. At this time, Whitby was the home of Caedmon, often called the father of English sacred song. He was an illiterate labourer, employed as cowherd and porter at the abbey. Caedmon had a vision in which great quantities of remarkable poetry revealed to him. The Abbess, Lady Hild, ordered that it should all be written down. Centuries later, the many cantos of Caedmon's Anglo-Saxon religious verse were still being sung in northern England and they exercised great influence on later English poets, especially Milton.

More than 1000 years later, Whitby had become an important whaling centre and James Cook (1728-1779) was born in the village of Marton, near Middlesborough,. He worked for a draper in Staithes, 11 miles north, and then became apprenticed to a local shipping firm. The house where he lodged with his master can be seen in Grape Lane. Later, he joined the Royal Navy and was rapidly promoted to a command, soon becoming Captain Cook – the name by which the world still knows him. He charted the coast of New Zealand and the eastern coast of Australia and was one of the greatest surveyors, as well as one of the finest sailors and explorers of all time. He learned his craft in Whitby vessels trading to the Baltic, and two of the vessels he used on his long and perilous voyages – Resolution and Endeavour were Whitby built. A bronze statue of the fa-

Whitby

mous circumnavigator was erected on the West Cliff and unveiled by Admiral Lord Charles Beresford on 2nd October 1912. The bi-centenary of Captain Cook's sailing on his first circumnavigation was celebrated in Whitby in August 1968, when a plaque of commemoration was unveiled by the High Commissioners of Australia and New Zealand.

Two other remarkable, but less-known Whitby navigators, were the William Scoresby's – a father and son, who added greatly to seafaring knowledge. Their interest was primarily in whaling, but they made careful observations of Arctic phenomena and invented several nautical instruments. Scoresby senior (1760-1829) pushed further through the pack-ice in 1806 than anyone had before; Scoresby Land, in east Greenland, and Scoresby Sound, are both named after his son.

But Whitby offers the visitor more than history; its situation is superb in the middle of one of Britain's most delightful stretches of coast, with cliffs and fine bays interspersed with picturesque fishing villages. The noble abbey may be a ruin, but the Parish Church of St

Mary, dating partly from 1110, and reached by 199 steps cut in the cliff, is still very much a part of the town. The church was originally of wattle and daub construction, later rebuilt in stone around 1110. The simple building, now enlarged was allowed to remain intact at the Dissolution in 1539. It has many interesting features including the Chomley pew, built in front of the chancel arch so that this well-to-do family could have the best view of the service. Other features include a triple-decker pulpit with a 'tester' canopy, box pews built in the 1600s that were rented out to the well-off with each family's name printed on the end, an Elizabethan altar, and many more.

Whitby Harbour

Although perhaps better known as a holiday resort and fishing town, Whitby has a long history as an industrial port. In the 16th century, alum, mined at Guisborough, was shipped through Whitby and coal was imported from Newcastle. By the 18th century Whitby was the sixth largest port in Britain and the centre of a shipbuilding industry, which continued until the early 1900s when ships of 6,000 tonnes were being launched. In recent times, there have been several visits by the replica of Cook's *Endeavour*, attracting large numbers of visitors to the small town.

Day Walk 1.The Washburn Valley and Dob Park

Distance: 8 miles

Parking: Swinsty Moor Plantation Car Park (Free)

Location: Map Ref. 186538 Off B6451 5 miles North Of Otley

Map: Explorer 297

Refreshments: Pubs – Timble Inn Timble, Sun Inn Norwood; café at Swinsty (weekends only)

Local Interest (see main text): Otley (historic market town etc) Bolton Abbey and Priory

---

A gentle stroll down part of the Washburn valley (Yorkshire's mini Lake District), returning via the superb Dob Park Bridge (packhorse bridge) and Dob Park Lodge. The route passes through old sheep farms and through Swinsty Moor Plantation to the ancient Swinsty Hall (see text). Please be aware that there are a number of difficult stiles on this route.

From Swinsty Moor Plantation car park cross the Fewston Embankment and turn right on to a foot path into woods at the end of the embankment. Follow the path at the side of the reservoir for just over a mile through a small car park and more woods coming out by the lodge building at the end of Swinsty Embankment. Take the path at the side of the building, heading down the embankment, and then follow the Washburn for the next 1½ miles through to Dob Park (Pack horse) bridge. Cross the bridge and take the track uphill past Middle Farm, then follow the main text from Dob Park House back to Fewston car park.

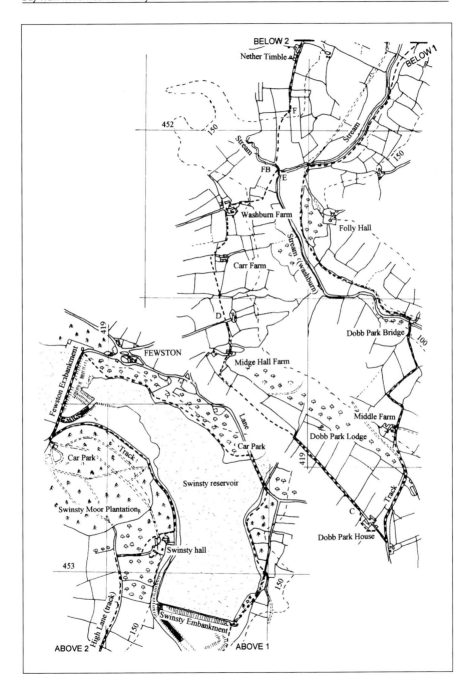

Day Walk 2. Pateley Bridge, Brimham Rocks and Nidderdale

Distance: 8 miles

Parking: Pateley Bridge (fee); Brimham Rocks (fee)

Location: Map ref. 158656 on the B6265, 16 miles west of Harrogate

Map: Explorer 298

Refreshments: pubs and cafés at Pateley Bridge, small refreshment kiosk at Brimham Rocks.

Local Interest (see main text): How Stean Gorge; Pateley Bridge (historic market town); Fountains Abbey; Stump Cross Caverns

Another gentle walk giving splendid panoramic views of Nidderdale along part of the Nidderdale Way, visiting the strange and wonderful rock formations at Brimham Rocks and returning via the meandering River Nidd to Pateley Bridge. There is one small climb from Fell Beck to Brimham rocks. From Pateley Bridge, follow the description in the main text as far as Brimham Rocks Visitors Centre.

Exit Brimham Rocks via the track at the side of the car park onto the lane. After 600m, turn right on a waymarked path, signposted 'Smelthouses' just before Mauds Farm. Follow the path/track steadily downhill for one mile, turning left at Low Wood House and onto a lane. Turn right downhill for 400m and left down a track at Smelthouses (just before Fell beck and the post box). Follow the track and cross the B6165 taking the waymarked footpath to the River Nidd. Turn right (up stream) and follow the river for the next 2½ miles back into Pateley Bridge via Glasshouses.

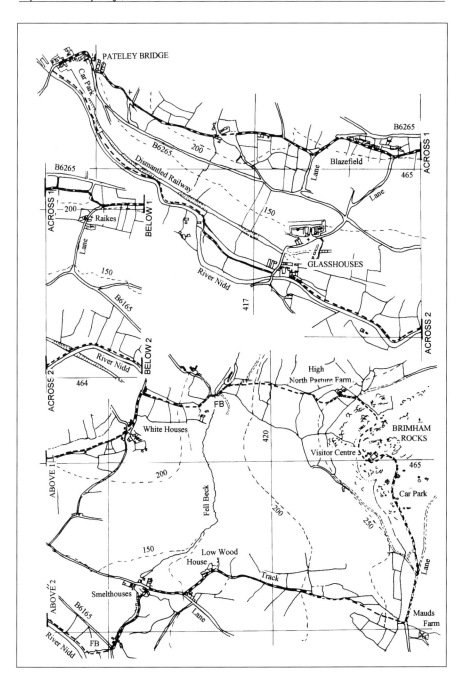

Day Walk 3. Fountains Abbey and Studley Royal Deer Park

Distance: 4 miles

Parking: Main Visitor Centre Car Park (Free)

Location: Map Ref. 273686. Off the B6265, four miles west of Ripon

Map: Explorer 298

Refreshments: Visitors Centre Café/Restaurant

Local Interest (see main text): Ripon (historic market town); Brimham Rocks; Pateley Bridge (historic market town)

This is a short walk on well-used paths with deer herds at Studley Royal and grand views of Fountains Abbey. Leave the car park via the track heading downhill. At the bottom of the hill, turn left onto the road and follow the main text from Fountains Abbey through Hill House Farm to the point F on the map. Turn left, downhill and after 300m left again by the stream. Follow the stream back through into Studley Royal Deer Park and then via the small path adjacent to the church back to the car park.

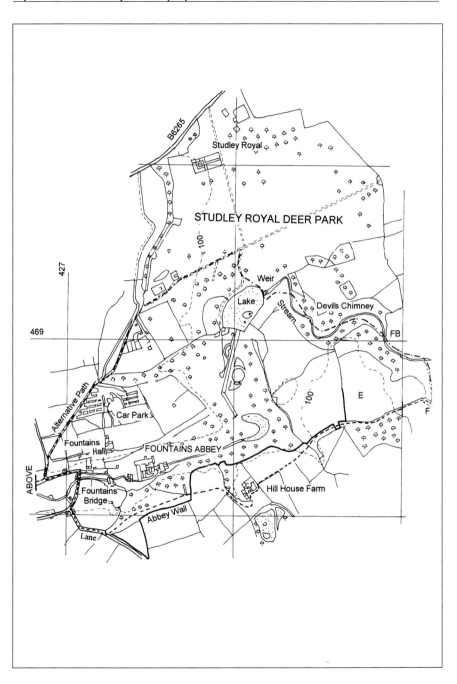

Day Walk 4. Byland Abbey and Kilburn

Distance: 6½ miles

Parking: Kilburn or Byland Abbey car park, both free

Location: Map ref. 513796. Off the A170, six miles east of Thirsk

Map: Outdoor Leisure 26

Refreshments: The Abbey Inn at Byland; Wombwell Arms, Wass; Black Swan, Oldstead; Foresters Arms, Kilburn. Café at Kilburn

Local Interest (see main text): White Horse of Kilburn, Rievaulx Abbey, Helmsley (Castle and market town)

A stroll through rolling farmland to Byland Abbey, returning via woodland and the Mount Snever Observatory with spectacular views over the Vale of York.

From Kilburn, follow the text through to the lane just before Wass and the Wombwell Arms. Turn left up the track through woods following the waymark sign to Cam Farm Observatory. Follow further waymark signs on forestry track coming out to a clearing. Turn right and follow the signs through to the observatory. Alternatively, to avoid the steep descent from the observatory, turn left and follow the forestry track. Pick up the waymark sign from the observatory after three-quarters of a mile. Mount Snever Observatory was built in 1838 to commemorate the coronation of Queen Victoria and is now disused. From the observatory descend to a forestry track, turning right and after 500m onto a tarmac lane at Oldstead. After 600m turn right into the farmyard at Scawling Farm and take the rough waymarked track into fields. After 600m cross a footbridge and turn right for Kilburn (signposted), carry straight on through gates onto a lane. Cross the lane and into High Kilburn following the original route back into Kilburn itself.

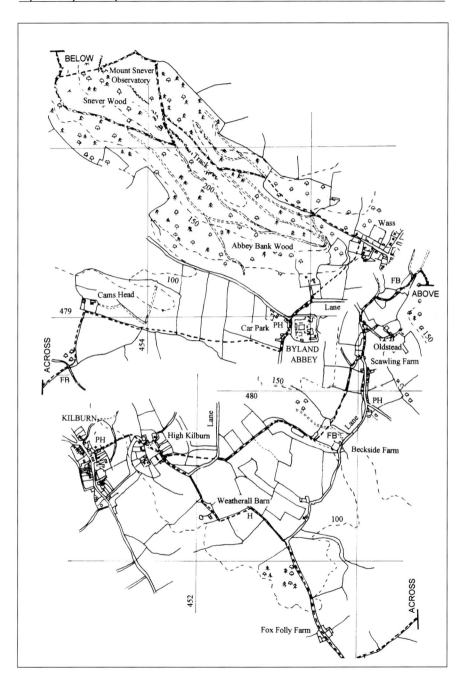

Day Walk 5. Rosedale Abbey, Rosedale and Old Mine Workings

Distance: 7½ miles

Parking: Rosedale (free)

Location: Map Ref.724959. Off the A170, eight miles north of Kirkbymoorside

Refreshments: There are two pubs and two cafés in Rosedale Abbey.

Local Interest (see main text): St Mary's Lastingham, Hutton-le-Hole, North York Moors

Another easy walk, following wooded streams and old mine haul-roads giving panoramic views down Rosedale. Disused mine workings are encountered with a return via ancient farm tracks.

Follow the main text up to the point where you would leave the haul-road (railway bed). Follow the waymark sign downhill to Dale Head Farm onto the lane for a few metres and then turn right on the waymarked path across the valley bottom and through to Moorlands Farm. At Moorlands Farm, follow the access road for 200m turning right onto Daleside Road (track). Follow the track for just over two miles to Thorgill, taking the waymarked path after High Thorgill Farm into the valley bottom. Cross the steam and follow the waymarked footpath along the valley, downstream, through a campsite back into Rosedale Abbey.

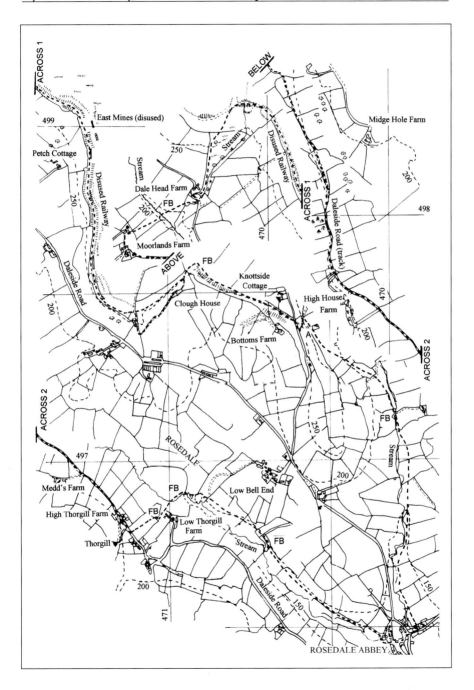

Appendices

Tourist Information

Otley – 0113 247 7707
Tourist Information Centre, Leeds City Council, Otley Area Office, 8 Boroughgate, Otley S21 3AH

Leeds – 0113 242 5242
Gateway Yorkshire, Leeds Tourist Information, PO Box 244, The Arcade, Leeds City Station, Leeds LS1 1PL

Pateley Bridge – 01423 711147
Tourist Information Centre, 14 High Street, Pateley Bridge, Harrogate HG3 5AW

Ripon – 01765 604625
Tourist Information Centre, Minster Road, Ripon HG4 1LT

Thirsk – 01845 522755
Tourist Information Centre, 49 Market Place, Thirsk YO7 1HA

Helmsley – 01439 770173
Tourist Information Centre, Town Hall, Market Place, Helmsley YO6 5BL

Pickering – 01751 473791
Tourist Information Centre, Ropery House, The Ropery, Pickering YO18 8DY

Whitby – 01947 602674
Tourist Information Centre, Langbourne Road, Whitby YO21 1YN

Market Town Information

	Market Days	Early Closing
Otley	Friday/Saturday	Wednesday
Pateley Bridge	n/a	Wednesday
Ripon	Thursday	Wednesday
Thirsk	Monday/Saturday	Wednesday

Map List

The current maps available for this walk are:

Explorer 288, Bradford & Huddersfield

Explorer 297, Lower Wharfedale and Washburn Valley

Explorer 298, Nidderdale

Explorer 299, Ripon & Boroughbridge

Explorer 302, Northallerton &Thirsk

Outdoor Leisure 26, North York Moors

Outdoor Leisure 27, North York Moors Eastern Area

Bibliography

Otley and District by Paul Wood, published by Allan Sutton Publishing Ltd.

Washburn Valley Yesterday by David Holred, published by Smith Settle.

Abbeys of Yorkshire by Colin Platt, published by English Heritage.

Medieval Monasteries of Great Britain by Lionel Butler and Chris Given Wilson, published by Michael Joseph.

The Abbeys and Priories of Medieval England by Colin Platt, published by Secker and Warburg, 1984, paperback.

The Yorkshire Nunneries in the 12th and 13th Centuries by Janet Burton, published by Borthwick Institute Publications.

Otley Historic Market Town Official Guide (from Otley Town Council)

St Mary's, Lastingham, published by Lastingham Parochial Church Council 1997.

Bewerley Grange Chapel by Muriel Swires, 1994; not published, but available from Beverley Grange.

Accommodation

Accommodation will have to be pre-planned with the relevant tourist board. For those wishing to walk the path using camping and Youth Hostels, the following information may be useful:

Otley

Camping

Stubbings Farm, Leeds Road: 01943 463087

Cowhead Farm, Askwith near Otley: 01943 463504

Pateley Bridge

Camping/caravan sites

Westfield Farm 01423 711410

Riverside Caravan Park 01423 711383

Low Wood Caravan Site 01423 711433

New Causeway Farm 01423 711422

Ripon

Camping/caravan sites

Birtree Parks, Ure Bank Caravan Park: 01765 602964 (Ripon Island)

Sawley Helgates Farm: 01765 620472

Clotha Holmes Farm: 01765 602818

Sawley Indhouse Farm: 01765 620276

Sawley Gowbusk Farm, Risplith: 01765 620212

Mr M. Bramley: 01765 690726

Thirsk

Camping/caravan sites

Thirsk Race Course: 01845 525266

Quernhow, Thirsk: 01845 567221

Thirkleby Hall Caravan Site: 01845 501630

Rievaulx
Camping:
Bungdale Head Farm: 01439 770589

Helmsley
Youth Hostel: Tel 01439 770433

Camping/caravan sites:
Foxholme Caravan and Camping Park at Helmsley: 01439 770416 or 771696 (but this is one and a half miles out of Helmsley)

Rosedale Abbey
Camping/caravan sites
W.C.P. & M. Doughty: 01751 417272
Rosedale Caravan and Camping Park: 01751 417272

Other
Neadham Meds Farm Cottage: 01751 417619

Whitby
Youth Hostel: Tel 01947 602878

Camping/caravan sites
Sandfield House Farm Caravan Park: 01947 602660
Stainsacre, Whitby: 01947 880430
North Cliff Holiday Park: 01947 880477

Car Parking
The following car parks are suitable for all-day parking:

Location	Size	Grid Ref.	Cost
Kirkstall Abbey	Large	259363	Free
Otley (Main Park)	Large	203457	Nominal Charge
Swinsty	Large	186538	Free
Fewston (A59)	Small	168533	Free
Thruscross	Large	154574	Free
Yorks Folly	Small	156637	Free
Pateley Bridge	Medium	158656	Charge
Brimham Rocks	large	208646	Charge

Fountains Abbey	Large	273686	Free
Ripon (Main Park)	Large	315713	Charge
Melmerby (Street Parking)	-	336768	Free
Thirsk (Market Place)	Medium	430821	Free
Kilburn	Small	513796	Free
Byland Abbey	Small	548790	Free
Rievaulx Abbey	Small	575849	Free
Helmsley (Market Place)	Medium	613837	Charge
Hutton–le–Hole	Large	705903	Charge
Rosedale Abbey (Street)	-	724959	Free
Glaisdale (Street Parking)	-	773054	Free
Grosmont	Large	825054	Charge
Sleights	Small	862082	Free
Whitby Abbey	Large	905111	Charge

Public Transport

For North Yorkshire bus and rail information, check www.ukbus.co.uk.

Train Information

All rail enquiries: 0345 484950

Glaisdale to Whitby is served by Arriva Trains Northern every 3½ hours – half-hour journey

Buses

Journey	Bus No	Every (mins)	Contact No.
Kirkstall to Otley	732	30	0113 245 1601
	733	30	0113 245 1601
	736	30	0113 245 1601
Otley to Harrogate	653	60	01274 734 833
Harrogate to Pateley Bridge	24	60	0160 978 0780 Ext 2372
Pateley Bridge to Killinghall	24	60	0160 978 0780 Ext 2372
Killinghall to Ripon	36A	60	0160 978 0780 Ext 2372
Ripon to Thirsk	70	60	0160 978 0780 Ext 2372
Thirsk to Easingwold	58	2½ hrs	0184 557 7250
Easingwold to Helmsley	31x	2 hrs	0134 783 8990
Helmsley to Glaisdale	North Yorks Moors bus, summer only		